113
1

The War in Afghanistan

by Richard Brownell

LUCENT BOOKS

A part of Gale, Cengage Learning

GALE
CENGAGE Learning™

Detroit • New York • San Francisco • New Haven, Conn • Waterville, Maine • London

LIBRARY OF CONGRESS CATALOGING-IN-PUBLICATION DATA

Brownell, Richard.
  The war in Afghanistan / by Richard Brownell.
    p. cm. -- (Hot topics)
  Summary: "The books in this series objectively and thoughtfully explore topics of political, social, cultural, economic, moral, historical, or environmental importance"-- Provided by publisher.
  Includes bibliographical references and index.
  ISBN 978-1-4205-0554-2 (hardback)
  1. Afghan War, 2001---Juvenile literature. I. Title.
  DS371.412.B76 2011
  958.104'7--dc23

                                                              2011021141

Lucent Books
27500 Drake Rd.
Farmington Hills, MI 48331

ISBN-13: 978-1-4205-0554-2
ISBN-10: 1-4205-0554-8

Printed in the United States of America
1 2 3 4 5 6 7 15 14 13 12 11

Printed by Bang Printing, Brainerd, MN, 1st Ptg., 09/2011

CONTENTS

FOREWORD

Young people today are bombarded with information. Aside from traditional sources such as newspapers, television, and the radio, they are inundated with a nearly continuous stream of data from electronic media. They send and receive e-mails and instant messages, read and write online "blogs," participate in chat rooms and forums, and surf the Web for hours. This trend is likely to continue. As Patricia Senn Breivik, the former dean of university libraries at Wayne State University in Detroit, has stated, "Information overload will only increase in the future. By 2020, for example, the available body of information is expected to double every 73 days! How will these students find the information they need in this coming tidal wave of information?"

Ironically, this overabundance of information can actually impede efforts to understand complex issues. Whether the topic is abortion, the death penalty, gay rights, or obesity, the deluge of fact and opinion that floods the print and electronic media is overwhelming. The news media report the results of polls and studies that contradict one another. Cable news shows, talk radio programs, and newspaper editorials promote narrow viewpoints and omit facts that challenge their own political biases. The World Wide Web is an electronic minefield where legitimate scholars compete with the postings of ordinary citizens who may or may not be well-informed or capable of reasoned argument. At times, strongly worded testimonials and opinion pieces both in print and electronic media are presented as factual accounts.

Conflicting quotes and statistics can confuse even the most diligent researchers. A good example of this is the question of whether or not the death penalty deters crime. For instance, one study found that murders decreased by nearly one-third when the death penalty was reinstated in New York in 1995. Death penalty supporters cite this finding to support their argument that the existence of the death penalty deters criminals from committing murder. However, another study found that states without the death penalty have murder rates below the national average. This study is cited by opponents of capital punishment, who reject the claim that the death penalty deters murder. Students need context and clear, informed discussion if they are to think critically and make informed decisions.

The Hot Topics series is designed to help young people wade through the glut of fact, opinion, and rhetoric so that they can think critically about controversial issues. Only by reading and thinking critically will they be able to formulate a viewpoint that is not simply the parroted views of others. Each volume of the series focuses on one of today's most pressing social issues and provides a balanced overview of the topic. Carefully crafted narrative, fully documented primary and secondary source quotes, informative sidebars, and study questions all provide excellent starting points for research and discussion. Full-color photographs and charts enhance all volumes in the series. With its many useful features, the Hot Topics series is a valuable resource for young people struggling to understand the pressing issues of the modern era.

INTRODUCTION

THE GRAVEYARD OF EMPIRES

The modern Muslim state of Afghanistan in southern Central Asia was founded in 1747. It is located in a harsh and desolate place, landlocked and mountainous, with volatile climates that include hot, dry summers in the south and severe winters in the highlands. There is not a great deal of vegetation, and the topography does not allow for vast agricultural production.

Afghanistan's history has been darkened by many years of warfare due to outside colonial influences and internal civil conflict. During this long history of strife, the residents of Afghanistan have maintained a fierce loyalty to their ethnic and tribal allegiances but not necessarily to the various governments that have ruled them. Outside forces that have sought to dominate the land over the centuries have often frustrated the desire of the Afghan people to be left alone. In fact, the nation's reputation for withstanding the sustained dominance of foreign powers has earned it the nickname "the graveyard of empires."

Throughout history, many nations have marched through Afghanistan, and the popular perception is that none of these conquerors were able to dominate the country. Anthropologist Thomas Barfield of Boston University believes, however, that the image of Afghanistan as a country that has resisted foreign dominance through the ages is incorrect. He points out that "until 1840 Afghanistan was better known as a 'highway of conquest.' For 2,500 years it was always part of somebody's empire, beginning with the Persian Empire in the fifth century B.C."[1] Alexander the Great, the Macedonian king who conquered the entire Persian Empire, conquered Afghanistan in 329 B.C., and although he died in 323 B.C., his successors managed to control much of the country for another two hundred years. Mongol Empire founder Genghis Khan, who was also rumored to have met his match in Afghanistan, actually devastated much of the country in his war of conquest in 1221.

A Pawn in a Great Game

During the nineteenth century, Afghanistan's geographical position as a gateway from Europe to India and the Far East brought it to the attention of both Great Britain and czarist Russia, two vast empires seeking to expand and solidify their territory. Their decades-long competition for control of the region was referred to as "The Great Game."

Great Britain invaded Afghanistan in 1836, and the first of three Anglo-Afghani wars followed. One famous story tells of there being one lone survivor of a sixteen-thousand-man British garrison after a battle with the Afghans. The second war started when the British returned in force in 1878. After two years of fighting, they occupied much of the country. The British held sway over Afghanistan until 1919, when, after a third war, the Afghans won their independence.

Afghanistan remained relatively stable for much of the twentieth century until a 1978 coup d'etat put the country in the hands of a regime allied with the Communist Soviet Union. The tyranny that followed destabilized the country, and the Soviets invaded on December 25, 1979, to prop up the regime and restore order.

The Soviet-Afghan War

Initially, Afghanistan's opposition to the Soviet invasion was weak. The Afghan fighters, collectively known as mujahideen, were Muslim guerrilla warriors from diverse regional groups that shared a devotion to Islam and opposition to occupation by the infidel Soviets. C.J. Dick of the Conflict Studies Research Centre, an independent policy group in Great Britain, writes, "The *Mujahideen* warrior fought for his family, his tribe and his religion. . . . Fighters were local men . . . [who] were untrained and necessarily part-timers."[2] The overwhelming Soviet force brutally wiped out Afghan opposition in the cities and tribal areas.

The United States, which attempted to stop the spread of communism and protect free nations, protested the Soviet invasion but initially did little else to stop it. Charles Wilson, a Democratic U.S. representative from Texas, took up the cause of the embattled Afghans. Wilson and Central Intelligence Agency (CIA) operative Gust Avrakotos developed a secret U.S. program to provide the Afghan guerrilla fighters with weapons and money to combat the Soviets.

Wilson and Avrakotos encountered opposition to their program in Congress and the American intelligence community. President Ronald Reagan's stated policy was to protect free peoples from Communist domination, but many U.S. bureaucrats did

Afghan mujahideen guerrilla fighters man an artillery position during the Soviet Union's invasion of Afghanistan in the 1980s.

not believe that Afghanistan was worth the effort. "The Afghans are hardly a people," stated Howard Hart, the CIA station chief in Pakistan, who was quite familiar with the region and its inhabitants. "They are a nation of tribes constantly at war with each other. They are very heterogeneous [diverse], with an extreme ethnocentricity [belief in their own tribe's superiority] which makes them not only hate or suspect foreigners but Afghans living two valleys away."[3]

Wilson used his considerable political connections in Washington and his diplomatic skills abroad to secure the money and the weapons needed to give the Afghans a fighting chance against the Soviets. Until Wilson came along in 1982, the mujahideen were being badly beaten in the field and were on the edge of total defeat. Soviet troops had superior firepower, and their helicopter gunships indiscriminately attacked Afghan soldiers and civilians alike, hitting towns, tribal gatherings, and convoys in the vast open stretches between districts.

Operation Cyclone, as the Wilson-Avrakotos effort became known, grew to become the largest CIA operation in the agency's history. The operation provided training and weapons to the mujahideen, but its most significant contribution was the introduction of the Stinger antiaircraft missile. This shoulder-fired weapon was used to great effect against the Soviet helicopters and helped turn the tide of the conflict.

Somewhere between five thousand and twenty thousand Muslim fighters came to Afghanistan from other countries to join the mujahideen in the struggle against the Soviets. The cause became known as a jihad (meaning a "holy struggle," originally against one's own sinful nature but in recent years, more often a fight against infidels, or non-Muslims—in this case, the Soviet troops). Among the foreign mujahideen was Osama bin Laden, the son of a wealthy Saudi businessman. Bin Laden followed a fundamentalist view of Islam that called for jihad against all foreigners in Muslim lands and a strict adherence to the teachings of the Prophet Muhammad. In 1988 he used his fortune to establish al Qaeda (meaning "the base"), an international network of fundamentalist Islamic fighters that would rely on violence to carry out Bin Laden's goals.

©1994 MAGELLAN Geographix℠Santa Barbara, CA (800) 929-4627

Aftermath of the Soviet Defeat

The Soviets admitted defeat and pulled out of Afghanistan in 1989. It was a great victory for Afghanistan and for the United States, but the peace was short-lived. Long-standing tribal feuds reignited. The battles were brutal and civilians were massacred by warring groups with U.S. weapons and training that had been intended to fight the Soviets. As the situation deteriorated, the United States became more reluctant to remain involved in Afghanistan. Diplomat Janet Bogue noted in late 1991 that "the U.S. government now finds itself giving guns to [the mujahideen] who [attack] civilian populations, and then we turn around and send in a humanitarian mission to deal with the refugees created by our own investment."[4]

When the Soviet Union collapsed in 1991, the half century of hostilities between the Soviet Union and Western nations known as the Cold War came to an end. The United States lost interest in Afghanistan. The far-off land no longer held any strategic importance. The arms shipments and CIA operations there ended. U.S. special envoy to Afghanistan Peter Tomsen thought this was a mistake. "U.S. perseverance . . . would sideline the extremists, maintain a friendship with a strategically located friendly country," he argued, adding, "We are in danger of throwing away the assets we have built up in Afghanistan over the last 10 years, at great expense."[5] Tomsen's message went unheeded. Many Americans were tired of the conflict and wanted to move on.

AFGHANISTAN BECOMES A TERRORIST HAVEN

Afghans suffered tremendous hardships during the Soviet war, and in 1990 the country was in a shambles. Over a million people had died. Six million refugees fled to neighboring Pakistan and Iran, many of them among the educated class. This resulted in a new generation of Afghans growing up in a country without enough teachers, intellectuals, businesspeople, or rational political figures to lead the way in developing a sustainable economic and civil order. Agriculture, the chief element of the economy, was severely damaged, leading to a national financial collapse. Additionally, land mines and unexploded bombs from the Soviet war littered the countryside, making roads impassable and farmland unusable. For years afterward it was not uncommon for innocent people to be maimed or killed by this leftover ordnance while going about their daily business.

In the aftermath of the Soviet withdrawal and America's subsequent pullout, Afghanistan became immersed in a violent struggle among competing factions to dominate the country. These tribes created their own autonomous regimes, sometimes ruling over the citizens in their region with brutal consequences. Justice was dispensed by whoever had the most firepower, and virtually any crime, no matter how minor, could be punishable by death.

The U.S. government faced accusations domestically and internationally that it was at least partly responsible for the chaotic situation in Afghanistan because of its withdrawal of support. Zalmay Khalilzad, a senior analyst at the Rand Corporation, an independent policy research group, argued that America's lack of engagement in the region was at fault. "After the fall of the Soviet Union, we stopped paying attention," Khalilzad wrote in the *Washington Post* in October 1996. "This was a bad decision. Instability and war in Afghanistan provided fertile ground for terrorist groups to train and hide. . . . Given the sacrifices made by the Afghans in the Cold War's final struggle, we had a moral obligation to assist them in achieving peace. We did not."[6]

When the Soviet army withdrew from Afghanistan in 1988, the country descended into a violent struggle between competing factions for control of the country.

Foreign affairs analyst Subodh Atal disagrees. He argues that if the United States had assisted Afghanistan after the Soviet war, it would have met the same fate as the Soviets did when they tried to reshape the country in their own image. "Any peace enforced at the point of the gun would have served to turn many of the Mujahideen factions against the United States. The U.S. military would have had to take sides in the competition among the irregular forces,"[7] he notes.

Atal's view suggests that the internal conflict in Afghanistan would have taken place regardless of America's actions. This assumption gains validity when considering the events that unfolded in Afghanistan in the years that followed.

The People of Afghanistan

Afghanistan contains numerous ethnic groups that are often remarkably dissimilar to one another. Some have their own language and their own standards of living and prefer to remain distinct from other ethnic groups. The largest ethnic group is the Pashtuns, accounting for about 40 percent of Afghanistan's 33 million people. They are concentrated largely in the south and east, along the Pakistan border, but also occupy several enclaves (distinct ethnic territories) around the country. They have been involved in the country's leadership since the eighteenth century, and they are the most politically powerful ethnic group.

The Tajiks of the northeastern portion of the country are the second-largest ethnic group. They are mostly farmers, but they are the dominant ethnic group in Afghanistan's largest cities. The Hazara occupy the rugged area of central Afghanistan, and since the nineteenth century they have often been either neglected or exploited by the more dominant Pashtuns. The Uzbeks are the last of the major ethnic groups, living in the north and sometimes among the Tajiks.

There is a complex tribal structure that exists within many, but not all, ethnic groups. Tribal affiliation is often determined by family genealogy and the ability to trace relations back to a common male ancestor. Some tribes have grown quite large over several generations, and they have developed smaller units referred to as subtribes. These groups are made up of people living in small communities in which everyone is familiar with one another and fiercely loyal to their group.

Tribes that share a common ethnic identity sometimes form alliances to seek common political goals. The Pashtuns, for example, contain two major groups of tribes. The Pashtun group known as the Durrani has been Afghanistan's dominant ruling group since 1747. The Ghilzai are generally poorer and less educated than the Durrani. Political agreement between these groups and among other tribes in Afghanistan has often proved difficult because of their cultural differences. Alliances can shift easily over even perceived insults to honor, and grudges are held for generations.

Some of the tribal leaders gain power and maintain control over the people through military force. Referred to as warlords, these leaders have been known to commit murder and other atrocities against their rivals. During the Soviet war, many warlords worked together to defeat the invaders, but they turned on each other afterward and created widespread violence.

Civil War

When the Soviets withdrew in 1989, the Communist government they had propped up was still in power. It did not have the broad support of the populace, though, because of its inability to bring an end to violence caused by the warlords. Dr. Mohammad Najibullah, who had been elected president in 1986, at first attempted to reconcile with the mujahideen, but they rejected his offer. The Soviets continued to provide Najibullah's government with the military equipment and economic aid he needed to stay in power. He achieved a military stalemate that kept the mujahideen temporarily in check, but defections weakened Najibullah's government. After the Soviet Union collapsed at the end of 1991, the vital aid he had come to rely on dried up.

Najibullah's government collapsed in April 1992, and he resigned from office. His victorious opponents signed a power-sharing agreement known as the Peshawar Accords. Under this arrangement, each of Afghanistan's major ethnic groups, including the Pashtuns and the Tajiks, would be represented in

Through the Peshawar Accords, Burhanuddin Rabbani was chosen to lead the new Afghan government. He attempted to hold general elections, but Pakistani-backed Hezb-i-Islami forces began a campaign to destabilize the interim government.

an interim government led by Burhanuddin Rabbani, the leader of Afghanistan's oldest political party, for a transitional period. This government attempted to initiate a process leading to national elections, but when Pakistan tried to install the more radical Islamist Gulbuddin Hekmatyar, as dictator in the capital city of Kabul, the agreement fell apart. (An Islamist is someone who advocates Islam as a political as well as a religious system).

Hekmatyar's Hezb-i-Islami forces, which included refugees who had fled to Pakistan during the Soviet war, started a bloody campaign that destabilized the interim government. They deliberately targeted civilians and killed thousands of people in their drive to take power and establish an Islamic state. Hekmatyar received operational and military support from the Directorate for Inter-Services Intelligence (ISI), the Pakistani intelligence agency, which was sympathetic to the fundamentalist Islamic cause that called for removal of infidels from Muslim lands and strict religious obedience. Islamic fighters from around the Middle East motivated by religious fervor also joined Hekmatyar.

In 1994 a group known as the Taliban (meaning "students") emerged in the southern city of Kandahar. The Taliban took their beliefs from a school of Muslim thought that sought to imitate the life and times of the Prophet Muhammad. This school of thought spread throughout the madrassas, or religious schools, of Pakistan and Afghanistan in the early 1990s. Under the direction of the mullah (a Muslim cleric) Mohammed Omar, the Taliban practiced a strict version of sharia—the sacred law of Islam—that rejected the inventions of the modern world and prohibited women from having any basic rights. They also had no tolerance for people who did not practice the Islamic faith, and they killed nonbelievers indiscriminately. Many religious scholars believed the Taliban incorrectly interpreted the words of the Koran, the principal Islamic text, and rejected their brand of Islam.

The Taliban took control of Kandahar and began a war of conquest that brought much of southern and central Afghanistan under their control. In May 1996 Hekmatyar accepted Rabbani's offer of a power-sharing agreement, and the Pakistanis abandoned him in favor of the Taliban. On September 27 the Taliban captured Kabul with the support of Pakistan and Osama bin Laden, who supplied money and weapons as well as fighters from his al Qaeda terrorist group.

THE "RESPECTED" TALIBAN

"I had an emotional attachment with the Taliban. They brought peace, they eradicated poppies, gave free education, medical treatment and speedy justice. They were the most respected people in Afghanistan."—Sultan Amir, Pakistan Consul General in Afghanistan

Quoted in Seth G. Jones. *In the Graveyard of Empires: America's War in Afghanistan.* New York: Norton, 2009, p. 64.

When the Taliban took over the capital in 1996, they established the Islamic Emirate of Afghanistan. They immediately began a war of extermination, wiping out entire villages that had supported their enemies. Hekmatyar and Rabbani fled the region, but former president Najibullah was captured by the Taliban and executed. Ahmad Shah Massoud, a popular Tajik hero in the war against the Soviets, charged with defending the Rabbani government, retreated north and established the Northern Alliance with leaders from several Afghan ethnic groups.

The Northern Alliance was the Western term given to the United Islamic Front for the Salvation of Afghanistan. This organization united numerous ethnic groups in fighting the Taliban. Massoud was the recognized leader, but he shared responsibility for protecting northern Afghanistan with Pashtun and Hazara groups as well as the Uzbeks, led by Abdul Rashid Dostum. Dostum had been allied with Hekmatyar in 1994, and he had fought with the Soviets against the mujahideen during the Soviet war. Massoud did not trust him, but they united against the threat of a common enemy.

The Taliban, with military and financial support from Bin Laden and the ISI, solidified their power through murder and intimidation. A 2001 United Nations (UN) report based on eyewitness accounts determined that the Taliban conducted fifteen separate massacres against civilians between 1996 and 2000, beating and shooting victims to death and dumping them in mass graves. The Taliban were able to draw some local support from the Pashtun areas of the south where the Taliban had originated. This allowed them to focus their efforts on defeating the Northern Alliance.

The Taliban continued their war against the Northern Alliance for the rest of the 1990s, and they defeated Dostum's forces in 1998. Dostum promptly fled the country. Massoud remained the only rival leader who stood in the way of the Taliban's control of all of Afghanistan. Massoud attempted a peace process with the Taliban, which they refused. Massoud likewise refused Taliban offers to join their government, figuring he would be murdered if he accepted. Afghanistan remained split between the two powers, with the Taliban controlling the lower 75 percent of the country. Massoud's moderate leadership earned him the loyalty of his followers. The U.S. and European governments recognized the Northern Alliance as the official government of Afghanistan.

Life Under the Taliban

The Taliban wasted no time in establishing their brand of radical Islam on the people under their control. The citizens of Afghanistan were indeed living a hard life after many years of warfare, but nothing could prepare them for what the Taliban had in store.

Mullah Omar and his followers transformed the country into what many observers compare to a medieval state. Almost every item of convenience or joy that Americans take for granted was banned. Television, music, movies, audio and videotapes, satellite dishes, VCRs, computers, cameras, photographs, art of any kind that depicted people, and even stuffed animals were

Pakistan Shields Osama bin Laden

On April 6, 2000, FBI director Louis Freeh traveled to Pakistan with conclusive proof that Osama bin Laden and al Qaeda in Afghanistan were responsible for the 1998 African embassy bombings. Freeh writes of the experience:

"I have some arrest warrants for bin Laden," I told the Pakistani leader [General Pervez Musharraf].

Musharraf laughed and asked me to tell him more. . . . He resisted my suggestion that we permanently base FBI agents in his country—even the moderate political parties would be upset by that he told me—but Musharraf readily agreed to let us send a second team . . . back to Pakistan to brief his staff in greater detail so they would know that our case was very factually based. Those briefings did take place, but in the end Musharraf refused to help. Taliban leader Mullah Omar, he said, had given his personal assurances that Osama bin Laden was innocent of the East African bombings and had abandoned terrorism. It was nonsense, but without Pakistan's assistance, Osama bin Laden was snug as a bug in a rug.

Louis J. Freeh. *My FBI: Bringing Down the Mafia, Investigating Bill Clinton, and Fighting the War on Terror.* New York: St. Martin's, 2005, p. 287.

gathered from the citizens and destroyed. Virtually every form of entertainment was prohibited. This included, but was not limited to, pool tables, board games, playing cards, dancing, flying kites, and applauding during whatever sporting events were still allowed.

Men were required to have a beard longer than a fist placed at the base of the chin. Conversely, they had to wear their hair short, and they were also required to wear a head covering. Women were reduced to a state of servitude not experienced in much of the world for centuries. They were segregated entirely from the male population, and they were not allowed to travel in public with anyone but a male relative. They were not allowed to congregate among themselves, and they were restricted to wearing burkas, a traditional form of dress that covered the

Afghan women wear burkas in Kabul. The Taliban reduced women to the point of servitude by forcing them to cover themselves completely and banning them from schools and workplaces.

entire body except for a small screen in front of the face to see out of. They could not wear makeup or high heels. Windows in their homes were painted over so they could not be seen from the outside.

LIFE FOR WOMEN UNDER THE TALIBAN

"[In 2000] UN rapporteur Kamal Hossain provided testimony about ethnic Hazara and Tajik women being rounded up in trucks and taken from the regions of Mazar-e-Sharif, Pol-e-Khomri and Shamali to neighbouring Pakistan and the Taliban stronghold of Kandahar.

"'Many suspect that women and girls end up forced into prostitution,' his report said, adding that 'women have been killed and maimed trying to escape from these trucks.'"—AFP News Agency

Quoted in AFP. "UN Report Flays Taliban Rights Violations Against Women in Afghanistan." March 9, 2000. www.rawa.org/un-reprt.htm.

Women were only allowed to be educated up to age eight, and the only jobs they could hold were in the medical sector. (Female doctors were needed because male doctors were not allowed to examine women.) This rule resulted in the closure of most public schools because women had dominated the teaching profession prior to the Taliban. Education not only disappeared as a profession but also as a practice. The madrassa teachers were often barely literate themselves, and there were few scholars with knowledge of Islamic law and history. Students brought up in the totally male society received little or no education in mathematics, science, history, or geography nor training in the traditional skills of farming or construction.

Punishment for any infraction of the Taliban rules was severe, with enforcement carried out by the Ministry for the Promotion of Virtue and Suppression of Vice. Theft was punished by the amputation of a hand, rape and murder by public execution, and adulterers were stoned to death. In Kabul, executions were often carried out in front of crowds in the city's soccer stadium.

Journalist Ahmed Rashid, author of *Taliban: Militant Islam, Oil and Fundamentalism in Central Asia*, suggests that Taliban leaders believed that "if they gave women greater freedom or a chance to go to school, they would lose the support of their rank and file."[8] Dominating women affirmed manhood, and the domination of women by the Taliban was a matter not only of principle but also of political survival.

Al Qaeda Finds a Home in Afghanistan

In 1996 Mullah Omar invited Osama bin Laden to use Afghanistan as a base of operations for training his al Qaeda warriors. This was in part a gesture of thanks for Bin Laden's support of the Taliban's takeover of much of Afghanistan. It also was a matter of prestige because Bin Laden had grown to almost mythic status among radical Islamic fundamentalists.

The purpose of al Qaeda was to fight and defeat the enemies of Islam, initially the Soviets, and later the United States and Israel, but also any nation or group that allied themselves with the "Great Satan," as the United States is often called by radical Islamic movements. Bin Laden had by 1996 gained international prominence for speaking out against the Saudi government when it supported the U.S. invasion of Iraq during the 1991 Persian Gulf War. He viewed the presence of the American military there as an insult to Islam punishable by death to the infidel troops. Bin Laden believed that the United States was responsible for the plight of poor Islamic peoples in the Middle East.

Because of his outspoken criticism of the Saudi government, Bin Laden's citizenship was revoked, and he moved to Sudan. While he was in Sudan, the al Qaeda network planned and executed a number of terrorist attacks against U.S. and non-Muslim military and civilian targets around the world. Members of al Qaeda were arrested in the United States for plotting to blow up New York City bridges, tunnels, and skyscrapers. Al Qaeda was also linked to the 1993 World Trade Center bombing, which killed four people and injured more than one thousand.

Bin Laden was expelled from Sudan in 1996, and he relocated to Afghanistan. He enjoyed star status there and was recognized as a key leader equal to Mullah Omar. Al Qaeda set up training camps and began recruiting Taliban members as warriors in its fight against the West. Omar recognized the power Bin Laden held over the people and gave him wide latitude to operate without interference.

On February 23, 1998, Bin Laden and Ayman al-Zawahiri, his Egyptian-born second-in-command, issued a fatwa (meaning "decree") calling on all Muslims around the world to kill Americans and their allies, civilians and military, "in order to liberate . . . [Mecca] from their grip, and in order for their armies to move out of all the lands of Islam, defeated and unable to threaten any Muslim."[9] The fatwa listed as reasons for this decree the continued U.S. military presence on the Arabian Peninsula, the intention of the American government to destroy the Muslim people of Iraq through economic sanctions, and the U.S. attempt to prop up Israel at the expense of the Arab states. Bin Laden contended that the United States fully intended to destroy the Islamic world by plundering the riches of Muslim lands and deposing their rulers for its own gain.

Al Qaeda's War Against the West

Al Qaeda and other terrorist groups that it supported had committed terrorist attacks against Western targets for years. These attacks consisted largely of assassinations, car bombings, and suicide attacks that were either poorly planned or limited in their effect. The establishment of al Qaeda's permanent base of operations in Afghanistan, together with Bin Laden's fatwa, significantly raised the stakes. George Crile, author of *Charlie Wilson's War*, suggests that the United States had a hand in creating this problem when it supported Afghanistan in the Soviet war: "The U.S. government sponsored the largest and most successful jihad in modern history. . . . The CIA secretly armed and trained several hundred thousand fundamentalist warriors. . . . Many of those who now targeted America were veterans of that earlier CIA-sponsored jihad."[10]

On August 7, 1998, truck bombs were exploded simultaneously at the U.S. embassies in Dar es Salaam, Tanzania, and Nairobi, Kenya. The death toll for both attacks was 223, with thousands wounded. Most of the casualties were local citizens, many of them Muslims. Twelve Americans were killed in the attacks.

On February 23, 1998, Osama bin Laden, right, and his second in command, Ayman al-Zawahiri, left, issued a fatwa, or decree, calling on Muslims around the world to kill Americans and their allies, both civilian and military.

The sophistication and violence of the attacks in Africa focused American attention on al Qaeda, particularly its leaders, Bin Laden and al-Zawahiri. They were now considered a significant threat to U.S. national security and therefore had to be dealt with. It was unclear, however, what methods could be used against this new enemy. Al Qaeda operated secretly in small groups in a number of locations. Bin Laden and al-Zawahiri were at the top of the command chain, but each group, or cell, operated completely independently of the other cells. Eliminating one cell would have no effect on the actions of the other cells. A U.S. intelligence official told the Cato Institute, a Washington, D.C., policy research organization: "The strength of the group is they don't need centralized command and control. Now, instead of a large, fixed target, we have little moving targets all over the world, all armed and all dangerous. It is a much more difficult war to fight this way."[11]

On August 20, 1998, U.S. president Bill Clinton ordered a series of cruise missile strikes in response to the bombings. American intelligence pointed to targets in Sudan and Afghanistan. In Sudan, the missiles destroyed the al-Shifa pharmaceutical factory, where 50 percent of Sudan's medications for both people and animals were manufactured. The Clinton administration claimed that there was ample evidence to prove that the plant produced chemical weapons, but a thorough investigation after the missile strikes revealed that the intelligence was unreliable.

Despite the failed effort, it was clear that al Qaeda must be stopped. An August 23 State Department cable noted that the United States had "reliable intelligence that the bin Laden network has been actively seeking to acquire weapons of mass destruction—including chemical weapons—for use against U.S. interests."[12] Clinton ultimately approved five separate intelligence orders authorizing secret action to destroy al Qaeda, but he never issued express orders to assassinate Bin Laden.

The Taliban's continued support of Bin Laden and his al Qaeda network inside Afghanistan created a firm link between the terrorists and Afghanistan in the eyes of the U.S. government. Clinton noted by executive order in July 1999 that "the actions and policies of the Taliban in Afghanistan, in allowing territory under its control in Afghanistan to be used as a safe haven and base of operations for Osama bin Laden . . . constitute an unusual and extraordinary threat to the national security and foreign policy of the United States."[13]

Al Qaeda struck again in October 2000 in a suicide attack against the USS *Cole*, a navy destroyer in the Port of Aden in Yemen. Seventeen U.S. sailors were killed and another thirty-nine were injured. President George W. Bush, who succeeded Clinton in 2001, authorized a plan on September 4 to go on the offensive against al Qaeda. The CIA would provide up to $200 million a year in material support to the Northern Alliance, the Taliban's sworn enemy, to do the job.

Some members of the Bush administration harbored concerns about whether the Northern Alliance would be a reliable ally. Massoud was popular, but other members in his command

The Persian Gulf War

On August 2, 1990, forces under the command of Iraqi dictator Saddam Hussein invaded and conquered the oil-rich emirate of Kuwait. The United States immediately condemned the unprovoked attack and assembled a coalition of nations to expel the Iraqi army. The American forces included 460,000 troops, fifteen hundred aircraft, and sixty-five warships in and around Saudi Arabia and other Persian Gulf nations. James T. Patterson briefly recounts the war, which began on January 15, 1991, in *Restless Giant: The United States from Watergate to* Bush v. Gore:

> The coalition attack featured two phases. The first entailed massive bombing of Kuwait, Baghdad, and other Iraqi cities and installations. This lasted 39 days. . . .

With Iraqi defenses rendered virtually helpless, coalition forces undertook the second stage. . . . In only 100 hours between February 23 and 27, this army shattered Iraqi resistance. . . . As Iraqi soldiers fled [from Kuwait] on February 27, [President George H.W.] Bush stopped the fighting. . . . Saddam Hussein . . . remained in control.

Needless to say, the decision to stop the fighting aroused controversy. . . . [Bush] insisted, however, that his exit strategy had always been clear: to free Kuwait and to drive Hussein back into Iraq. "I do not believe," Bush said later, "in what I call 'mission creep,'" or the extension of operations beyond the original stated goal.

James T. Patterson. *Restless Giant: The United States from Watergate to Bush v. Gore.* New York: Oxford University Press, 2005, pp. 232, 233, 234.

U.S. planes bomb Baghdad on the night of January 15, 1991. The attack was in response to Saddam Hussein's invasion of Kuwait.

structure were considered to be thugs, and several were accused of human rights violations. Additionally, the Taliban forces outnumbered those of the Northern Alliance almost two to one. Massoud was assassinated by al Qaeda operatives on September 9, 2001, dealing a significant blow to the Northern Alliance. U.S. planners recognized this event as troubling, but the next day, Condoleezza Rice, Bush's national security adviser, prepared a directive for the president to sign to begin the operation anyway.

September 11

Early the next morning, however, on September 11, 2001, Muslim hijackers flew two American passenger jets into the Twin Towers of the World Trade Center in New York City. Another jet was hijacked and flown into the Pentagon in Arlington, Virginia. A fourth hijacked jet, presumably meant to crash into either the White House or the U.S. Capitol, crashed instead in a field in Shanksville, Pennsylvania, after passengers fought the hijackers to regain control of the plane.

Both 110-story towers of the World Trade Center along with the five surrounding buildings of the complex were completely destroyed, killing 2,753 people, including 147 on the planes, which were obliterated on impact. At the Pentagon, 184 people were killed, including 59 airline passengers. Forty people died in the Shanksville crash.

Two weeks before the attacks, John O'Neill, a counterterrorism expert and retired assistant director of the FBI, had accepted the position of director of security at the World Trade Center. On September 10, 2001, O'Neill told two of his friends, "We're due. And we're due for something big. . . . Some things have happened in Afghanistan. . . . I don't like the way things are lining up in Afghanistan. . . . I sense a shift, and I think things are going to happen . . . soon."[14] O'Neill died on September 11 when the South Tower collapsed.

In the days that followed, while the nation reeled from the most devastating attack ever committed on American soil, U.S. intelligence officials gathered evidence to determine who was responsible for the attacks. Based on the evidence that was available, authorities in the United States quickly asserted that

Osama bin Laden and his al Qaeda organization were solely responsible, and other suspects were ruled out. The British government separately reached the same conclusion. Although he denied the attacks at first, Bin Laden later claimed responsibility.

President Bush made a speech to a joint session of Congress and the American people on September 20. He announced to the nation that the United States would bring justice to the terrorists and those who harbored them. He also spoke directly to the leaders of Afghanistan:

> The United States of America makes the following demands on the Taliban: Deliver to United States authorities all the leaders of al Qaeda who hide in your land. Release all foreign nationals, including American citizens, you have unjustly imprisoned. Protect foreign journalists, diplomats and aid workers in your country. Close immediately and permanently every terrorist training camp in Afghanistan, and hand over every terrorist, and every person in their support structure, to appropriate authorities. Give the United States full access to terrorist training camps, so we can make sure they are no longer operating.
>
> These demands are not open to negotiation or discussion. The Taliban must act, and act immediately. They will hand over the terrorists, or they will share in their fate.[15]

Mullah Omar flatly refused Bush's ultimatum. America's course of action was now clear.

CHAPTER 2

OPERATION ENDURING FREEDOM BEGINS

The Taliban's refusal to turn over Bin Laden and the members of al Qaeda in Afghanistan set the United States on a course for war. Many U.S. allies, including the United Kingdom and several other nations, pledged support to the United States in removing the Taliban and al Qaeda. The North Atlantic Treaty Organization (NATO), an international defense organization based in Belgium, invoked Article 5 of its charter for the first time in its fifty-two-year history. Article 5 states that an attack on any NATO member country would be considered an attack on all member countries, and that all members would act in mutual defense. There was a certain irony to this action in that Article 5 was originally intended to clear the way for the United States to protect its weaker allies from aggression, yet the first time it was ever invoked was in the defense of the mightiest member of the alliance.

The United States began planning a military response as soon as it was certain that Afghanistan was the target. The mission to overthrow the Taliban and al Qaeda was named Operation Enduring Freedom, and it would include air strikes, covert operations, and ground fighting alongside the Northern Alliance. The British pledged military support and joined the invasion. Operation Veritas (Latin, meaning "truth"), the British codename for the operation, would be planned by British forces, but in close coordination with U.S. leadership.

American military planners recognized that they faced several challenges in toppling the Taliban and eliminating al Qaeda. The old belief that Afghanistan was the graveyard of empires

NATO's Operation Enduring Freedom against the Taliban included air strikes, covert operations, and fighting on the ground alongside the Northern Alliance.

surfaced once again, and there was great concern that America could get dragged into a prolonged conflict. The situation called for a military campaign unlike any the United States had ever fought.

Challenges to the U.S. Mission

The U.S. government and military had to take several other important factors into account in the planning and execution of the Afghanistan invasion. Chief among the concerns of military leaders were the country's terrain and its inhabitants. Seth G. Jones, author of *In the Graveyard of Empires: America's War in Afghanistan*, writes, "The terrain and conditions were unlike anything the Americans had ever seen." For example, U.S. military personnel "found themselves traversing steep mountain paths next to thousand-foot precipices."[16] Since vehicles could not negotiate these trails, U.S. soldiers had to rely on horses, and many had no experience in horse riding.

Afghanistan was landlocked, which meant that U.S. forces could not bring in troops via naval vessels. They would need to obtain permission from neighboring countries for basing and fly-over rights. Uzbekistan, Turkmenistan, and Tajikistan, all to the north, were former Soviet republics still under the influence of Russia. The Russians and these nations were willing to offer bases for American troops, but the Russians were wary of providing the United States long-term permission to put troops in the territory. To the south, it was known that Pakistan was sympathetic to the Taliban and that the ISI embraced radical Islamic beliefs. The Pakistani government of General Pervez Musharraf was willing to let the United States use its bases as a staging area, but it was unclear to what extent his government could be trusted.

The United States believed it had found an ally in the Northern Alliance, but the alliance was made up of a coalition of tribes and regional groups. Allegiances shifted easily among Afghan groups, and money could easily buy the support of any tribal leader. Some groups had been infiltrated by al Qaeda agents, and others had been bought off by the Taliban, only to be later bought off by the Americans for more money. Trust was not easy to come by in a land where loyalty went to the highest bidder. Also, Afghan fighters often refused to fight at night, which made pursuit of fleeing enemy forces difficult. One troubling aspect of the Afghan fighters that American forces discovered in the field was that, after a victorious battle, they would often loot the dead and steal weapons and other items. It was hard to build morale and maintain order under these circumstances. It was also difficult to hold conquered territory because after their looting spree, Afghan fighters would often flee, sometimes never to be seen again. Delta Force commander Dalton Fury writes, "Beyond getting the Taliban off their necks, the Afghan military and tribal leaders had goals that were much different than our own."[17]

The forces of al Qaeda were entrenched in various pockets in the mountainous regions of Afghanistan. U.S. forces could not easily spot them, nor could they easily target them because it was difficult for American pilots to determine on sight who was friend or foe. Widespread bombing was ruled out as ineffective because al Qaeda forces were widely dispersed.

CALLING FOR PEACE

"We feel this conflict can be solved peaceably; we don't need to use more violence. We have international standards. We don't need to attack the Afghan people."—Mairead Maguire, peace activist and Nobel Peace Prize winner

Quoted in Robert Worth. "In Three Languages, Urgently Chanting for Peace." *New York Times*, October 8, 2001, p. B12.

There were also questions in the international community about the legitimacy of U.S. actions. Professor Marjorie Cohn of the Thomas Jefferson School of Law in San Diego noted that a U.S. bombing campaign against Afghanistan would be illegal, because the UN Security Council, of which the United States is a member, is the only international body that can authorize the use of force, and it did not do so. The Bush administration countered that UN Security Council authorization was not required since the invasion was an act of collective self-defense provided for under Article 51 of the UN Charter. This article states, "Nothing in the present Charter shall impair the inherent right of individual or collective self-defence if an armed attack occurs against a Member of the United Nations, until the Security Council has taken measures necessary to maintain international peace and security."[18] But, according to Cohn, "the bombing of Afghanistan is not legitimate self-defense under article 51 of the Charter because: 1) the attacks in New York and Washington D.C. were

The Life of an American Soldier in Afghanistan

U.S. soldiers faced harsh living conditions while serving in Afghanistan. First Sergeant R. Levis of the 377th Parachute Field Artillery served with Task Force Geronimo from October 2003 near Khost in eastern Afghanistan. He explains the situation:

> Soldiers were sleeping in the one-man tents. . . . In other words, soldiers had nowhere to go to get out of the heat or to relax. Bottled water was the only water we had and monitored closely to ensure that we did not run out. The only hygiene that could be allowed was brushing teeth and shaving. We only had what we could carry in our ruck sacks, so everyone had only one change of Desert Camouflage Uniform and four changes of under clothes. A gutted out port-a-potty served as the only latrine.

This latrine had a can slipped in from the back which of course had to be burned twice daily. Burning the waste raised another issue, fuel. The only fuel we had, had been carried in five gallon cans on the vehicles and due to the weight, we could not bring an abundance of it with us.

> The only electricity that we had came from the 5k generator that we had brought with us. That was only used to charge batteries and keep the communications equipment powered up. Soldiers could not use it for any other personal items. The heat was intense and there was no relief from it until the sun went down. There were no air conditioners or even a fan. [Meals Ready to Eat] were our only meals which was enough to lower any person's morale. Mail was almost nonexistent.

U.S. Army Sergeants Major Academy et al. *Long Hard Road: NCO Experiences in Afghanistan and Iraq.* Ft. Belvoir, VA: Defense Technical Information Center, 2007, p. 68.

American soldiers return to their tent barracks at Bagram Air Base in Afghanistan. U.S. forces battled the harsh conditions, including the heat and terrain, as much as they battled the Taliban.

criminal attacks, not 'armed attacks' by another state, and 2) there was not an imminent threat of an armed attack on the U.S. after September 11, or the U.S. would not have waited three weeks before initiating its bombing campaign."[19]

The argument of legitimacy was further complicated because the Bush administration did not seek a declaration of war from Congress, as required by the Constitution. In the confusion over the terms of warfare, Taliban troops were labeled as supporters of terrorists rather than soldiers, which denied them protection as lawful combatants under the Geneva Convention, an international treaty that set standards for the treatment of victims and combatants in war.

American Troops Confront Battlefield Obstacles

On October 7, 2001, the invasion began with U.S. and British air strikes against known Taliban and al Qaeda positions. Bombers operating at high altitudes well out of range of antiaircraft guns attacked al Qaeda training camps and Taliban air defenses.

The strikes initially focused on the area in and around the major Afghan cities of Kabul, Jalalabad, and Kandahar. Within a few days, most al Qaeda training sites were severely damaged and the Taliban's air defenses were destroyed. U.S. aircraft, including Apache helicopter gunships from the 101st Combat Aviation Brigade, operated without losses throughout the campaign because they had completely wiped out the meager Taliban air defenses. The campaign then focused on command, control, and communication targets, which weakened the ability of the Taliban forces to coordinate their own defenses.

The air campaign was fairly straightforward in its approach. There were a number of specific targets that needed to be eliminated. On the ground, however, U.S. military strategists debated over a number of strategies. U.S. forces could invade the south, but that was where the Taliban were strongest and that meant running the risk of high casualties. Invading the north and joining the Northern Alliance was politically risky. A victorious Northern Alliance would be stronger than the Pashtun groups fighting to the south, fracturing the delicate political and ethnic balance that existed among the opponents of the Taliban. This could split the country and lead to civil war in a post-Taliban Afghanistan. Another option was not to put any American soldiers on the ground and to provide support for anti-Taliban fighters from afar. A ground battle between anti-Taliban fighters and the Taliban and al Qaeda forces could take a long time, however, and its outcome was far from assured.

U.S. planners agreed that small teams of U.S. special forces units consisting of Delta Force, Army Rangers, and Navy SEALs would infiltrate the country and link up with Afghan resistance fighters. Their mission was to target, capture, or kill high-value Taliban and al Qaeda personnel. A principal task of these special forces was to call in air strikes on Taliban and al Qaeda positions that could only be identified on the ground. These close operations were dangerous because American soldiers were often calling down bombs on positions that were close to their own location. There was no room for error, but friendly-fire accidents did take place. Delta Force commander Dalton Fury explains: "No one could tell us on a map where anyone was located, and everyone looked alike, so how could the bomber and fighter pilots be blamed for any confusion? They were doing their best with the information they had. . . . Unfortunately, America lost face with our allies every time it happened."[20]

THE RIGHT THING TO DO

"We've been looking forward to the U.S. taking action. But we think the attack is not on regular citizens, and so all and all it is a positive thing, a new beginning for our people."—Ekliel Mohmand, an Iraqi immigrant living in New York

Quoted in Daniel J. Wakin and Charlie LeDuff. "Among New York Muslims, Support for U.S. Strikes." *New York Times*, October 8, 2001, p. B11.

Special forces groups operated differently than conventional U.S. military forces in that they worked in small units, and they were completely self-sustaining. These units were trained to be deployed deep in enemy territory under hostile conditions. The secrecy of their mission meant that they would have little, if any, access to outside resources. They were independent and untraceable in the field. Communications with headquarters were informative, but often brief, and sometimes off schedule. Master Sergeant D. Barry of the Airborne Third Special Forces Group explains how the units operated: "NCOs (noncommissioned officers) of the team drive forklifts to load equipment, medical needs are conducted by the team medic, the team engineer conducts supply issues. We develop our own intelligence briefs with the Intelligence NCO and the Assistant Detachment Commander."[21]

In the North, U.S. special forces consisting of three twelve-man teams linked up separately with Northern Alliance generals who had only a few years earlier fought the ground battle against Taliban and al Qaeda personnel in the cities of Mazar-i-Sharif and Kabul, the Afghan capital city.

The CIA had not been able to establish contacts in the Pashtun tribal belt in the south like they had in the north. Much of the American focus was on aiding the Northern Alliance, but the U.S. units had to be careful to maintain balance among the four major ethnic groups—Pashtuns, Tajiks, Hazaras, and Uzbeks—throughout the country. If any of the ethnic groups believed that they were being given less support than any of the others, the whole anti-Taliban alliance might degenerate into infighting and collapse. Captain Jason Amerine, the special forces commander in the south, worried that not enough thought had been put into the strategy behind his group's infiltration. His concerns are voiced by Eric Blehm, author of *The Only Thing Worth Dying For*: "There was no master plan for Afghanistan. The entire military campaign for the southern half of the country had to be shaped by the first Americans to infiltrate the region."[22]

In the south, eleven members of the U.S. special forces linked up with Pashtun tribal leaders allied with Hamid Karzai. Karzai came from a respected family allied with the royalist faction that had ruled Afghanistan for many years before the Soviet invasion. He was educated in the West and was often considered even-tempered and above the ethnocentric views embraced by other Afghan politicians. He had also long been an outspoken critic of the Taliban.

Flight of the Taliban

U.S. combat forces and Northern Alliance fighters captured the city of Mazar-i-Sharif on November 9. This was a strategic victory because the city was a major transportation hub, with two airports and a supply route into neighboring Uzbekistan, where larger U.S. forces were gathering. It was also a major symbolic victory because it was home to a sacred Muslim site known as the Blue Mosque, said to be one of the burial places of Ali, cousin and son-in-law of the Prophet Muhammad. It also enabled humanitarian aid organizations to access the country in their ongoing attempts to alleviate Afghanistan's looming food crisis, which had threatened more than 6 million people with starvation. Many of those in most urgent need lived in rural areas to the south and west of Mazar-i-Sharif.

Taliban forces fled the city of Kabul during the night of November 12. By the time Northern Alliance forces arrived on the afternoon of November 13, they found the charred remains of Taliban gun emplacements. The fall of Kabul marked the beginning of a collapse of Taliban positions across the country. The next day, all the Afghan provinces along the Iranian border, including the key city of Herat, had been conquered by allied forces. Taliban holdouts in the north, mainly radical Islamic Pakistanis, fell back to the northern city of Kunduz to make a last stand. The Northern Alliance wiped out the Taliban's last position in northern Afghanistan on November 16.

By the end of November, the remaining ten thousand Taliban fighters who refused to surrender had been forced back to Kandahar, the first city they had ever controlled in Afghanistan. It was now their last remaining stronghold, and it came under increasing pressure. Karzai led three thousand tribal fighters from the east and cut off the northern Taliban supply lines to Kandahar. The Northern Alliance forces closed in from the north and northeast.

U.S. combat troops arrived in force on November 25, establishing a base in the desert south of Kandahar. This was the first major military deployment in Afghanistan since the beginning of combat operations nearly two months previously.

As the Taliban fled Kabul, Northern Alliance troops took the capital on November 12, 2001.

Air strikes continued to pound Taliban positions inside the city, where Mullah Omar had barricaded himself. He remained defiant despite the fact that the Taliban now only controlled four of the thirty Afghan provinces, and he called on his forces to fight to the death. Karzai wanted to offer amnesty to Omar, but the United States refused. While some Taliban fighters stalled for time, pretending to negotiate for a cease-fire, Omar slipped out of Kandahar on December 7 with his most hardcore loyalists. Many of the remaining Taliban fighters fled into the mountains of southern Afghanistan.

Tora Bora

Prior to the fall of Kandahar, while the rest of Afghanistan was rapidly falling under the control of American and allied forces, Bin Laden and his remaining al Qaeda fighters fled to Tora Bora, a rugged mountainous region that consisted of an intricate complex of caves on the Pakistan border, to prepare for a stand against the Northern Alliance and American and British forces. By mid-November 2001, nearly two thousand al-Qaeda and Taliban fighters had fortified themselves within the caves.

Dalton Fury, the senior American commander in Tora Bora, describes the region. "It is a vertical no-man's land, a hellish place of massive, rocky, jagged, unforgiving snow-covered ridgelines and high peaks separated by deep ravines and valleys studded with mines."[23]

U.S. special forces and British Special Air Service commando teams infiltrated the area on December 3. They called in U.S. air strikes to open a path for tribal fighters, who began the ground invasion on the fortress on December 5. Several al Qaeda fighters who survived the bombardment and the fighting approached tribal militia about a cease-fire, which Afghan general Hazrat Ali accepted on December 12. U.S. forces insisted on moving forward. Commander Fury believed that Bin Laden was in their grasp. His team had been monitoring Bin Laden's transmissions, which Fury regarded as increasingly desperate. The last one the U.S. forces intercepted on December 13 recorded Bin Laden saying, "Our prayers were not answered. Times are dire and bad. We did not get support from the apostates, who are our brothers. I'm sorry for bringing you here. It is okay to surrender."[24]

The Americans continued the assault. The last cave complex was taken on December 17, but a subsequent search did not turn up Bin Laden or his leadership among the two hundred dead al Qaeda fighters. Fury and many other military experts believed at the time that Bin Laden slipped away into the mountains of Pakistan during the cease-fire. The fact that Bin Laden

Northern Alliance troops wait in front of Tora Bora as American B-52s drop bombs on Taliban positions. American and Northern Alliance forces took Tora Bora on December 17, 2001. Osama bin Laden escaped.

had survived Tora Bora was not conclusively proved until October 2004 when he created a video message that was released by Al Jazeera, the Arabic news agency.

Debating the Next Steps in the U.S. Mission

U.S. and coalition forces effectively controlled much of Afghanistan by the end of 2001, although fighting continued as they worked with Afghan forces to consolidate their gains. Where Bin Laden was hiding, if he was even still alive, was but one question now facing the planners of Operation Enduring Freedom. Afghanistan, shattered from years of war, was badly in need of a new government and international aid that could rebuild the country, but there were questions as to how large a role the United States should play in rebuilding Afghanistan.

Nation building is a foreign policy term that describes the process by which one nation or a group of nations works to develop a poor or fractured state into a politically stable and unified member of the international community. Paul Miller, professor of international security studies at the College of International Security Affairs at the National Defense University, explains: "Nation building is an investment in future allies and a means of balancing against potential rivals. Part of U.S. grand strategy is (or ought to be) the effort to prevent rival powers . . . from amassing enough power to seriously threaten our way of life."[25] Miller and other supporters of nation building believe that it is necessary to engage in such a process in Afghanistan in order to prevent the country from once again becoming a terrorist haven. Their argument is that if the United States simply left Afghanistan after defeating the Taliban and al Qaeda, these elements would return, and the American war effort would have gained nothing. The world would be no safer from terrorism than it was before September 11.

Nation building as a means of defense has supporters and critics among U.S. policy makers. Former national security officials for the Bill Clinton administration Ivo Daadler and James Lindsay argue that the process should be applied across the globe in order to defeat terrorism. "We must intensify our efforts to resolve conflicts around the world, and especially in the

Middle East. . . . We must also intensify support for democracy and promote economic development—especially in areas like Central Asia, the Arab world, and northern Africa."[26] Skeptics of this approach believe the financial, military, and human costs of such an effort are too high. Gary Dempsey, a foreign policy analyst at the Cato Institute, a libertarian policy research organization, notes, "Osama bin Laden's Al Qaeda organization . . . reportedly has operations in 68 countries. . . . How many of those countries should be targeted for nation building?"[27] Such an effort is clearly beyond the capabilities of the United States.

In Afghanistan in particular, U.S. policy planners remain concerned about an extended American presence in the country. Extended nation building efforts require a stable security situation in which aid workers and groups tasked with efforts such as building roads and public services can freely and safely operate. Afghanistan remains a very dangerous place despite the gains made in late 2001. Introducing more Americans into that environment and keeping them there for extended periods of time raised safety risks and added to local hostilities. Subodh Atal writes, "One of the many perils of nation building is that, despite the best intentions and efforts of the foreign powers, the local population starts to resent its presence."[28]

One major concern for U.S. policy planners has been whether Afghanistan is even suited for a national government. The deep roots of the various ethnic groups and the complex tribal structure in much of the country indicate that it may be impossible to create one national government. If a national government is not suitable, an alternative would be a federation of semiautonomous regions each governed by the predominant ethnic group of that area.

Most policy experts agreed that, irrespective of what type of government ultimately ruled Afghanistan, the United States should not dictate that choice. They predicted that if the Afghan people perceived that America had installed the country's government, they would have no respect for it, and they would view the United States as occupiers rather than liberators. Dempsey, reminding America of its stated goals, argues, "The security of the United States does not require a multiethnic, liberal democracy

Pat Tillman

[Pat] Tillman was far from a household name when he put aside his NFL career to enlist in the U.S. Army eight months after the 9/11 attacks. But at a time when there was a lot of high-minded talk about the price of freedom, Tillman quickly captured the nation's attention as the most vivid example of all those who were actually willing to walk the walk. Just married to his high-school sweetheart, forsaking a $3.6 million contract extension offer from the Arizona Cardinals, Tillman was giving up an extremely enviable life to serve his country. That he understood his decision to do so made him no nobler than anyone else who'd done the same—and therefore refused to speak publicly about his enlistment—only added to his appeal. . . .

On April 22, 2004, less than two weeks after Tillman and his younger brother Kevin had deployed to Afghanistan—he'd done his initial tour of duty in Iraq—Tillman was shot three times in the head by one of his fellow Rangers. . . .

Instead of conveying this inconvenient truth, however, the Army announced that Tillman had been killed by enemy fire during a chaotic exchange that had involved as many as a dozen enemy combatants. . . .

Tillman's family pursued the truth behind his death for several years, and in the investigations that followed, high-ranking Pentagon officials all the way up to Secretary of Defense Donald Rumsfeld were implicated in the cover up.

Greg Beato. "The Pat Tillman Story." *Reason*, September 16, 2010. http://reason.com/archives/2010/09/16/the-pat-tillman-story.

Former National Football League star Pat Tillman was killed by friendly fire in Afghanistan. The army initially covered up the incident, saying that Tillman had been killed by enemy fire.

in Afghanistan. It requires only that the government or governments there be deterred from harboring terrorists as the Taliban once did."[29]

The debate within the U.S. government of how or whether to engage in nation building in Afghanistan would continue even after the United States had clearly begun the process. At the very least, it was agreed by the United States and its coalition allies that a new government had to be established.

CHAPTER 3

ATTEMPTING TO REBUILD AFGHANISTAN

Afghanistan had not experienced peace or a nationally recognized government since before the Soviet invasion of 1979. Decades of conflict had left the country without the basic functions that a stable government can provide. Security for the citizenry was virtually nonexistent; there was no judicial system, and much of the country lacked water and food services, electricity, medical facilities, and schools. In this environment, the public had little if any faith in governing institutions. The U.S.-led coalition recognized that the first priority in rebuilding Afghanistan would have to be setting up a government that would not only meet the needs of the Afghan people but also earn their trust.

This was no easy task. Afghanistan consisted of a number of ethnic groups that each had their own loyalties and goals. Gary Berntsen and Ralph Pezzullo, authors of *Jawbreaker: The Attack on Bin Laden and Al Qaeda*, write, "Afghanistan truly is a zero sum game. Anytime anyone advances all others consider this to be at their expense."[30]

This obstacle was but one reason that opponents of nation building weighed in against the United States becoming too heavily involved in post-Taliban Afghanistan. They also argued that policy planners were vastly underestimating the extent of the task that lay ahead. The war-torn country had been ravaged by conflict for so long, few citizens could even recall what a peaceful Afghanistan looked like. According to Malou Innocent and Ted Galen Carpenter of the Cato Institute, "Rather than re-building, the United States and NATO would be building much of the country from scratch, such as erecting infrastructure and tailoring a judicial system to make it both 'modern' and compatible with local customs."[31]

Establishing a Government

Politics in Afghanistan has historically consisted of power struggles, bloody coups, and unstable and unpredictable transfers of power. The concept of creating a democracy consisting of elected leaders was challenging both to the Afghans and the international community. The UN, which condemned the terrorist attacks on the United States but did not endorse the U.S. military response in Afghanistan, took up the task of building a new government for the country.

Lakhdar Brahimi, the special representative of the secretary-general of the UN, became the point person for organizing a gathering of political figures who would debate and develop the government. Brahimi, an Algerian, was a respected envoy with a long career in the diplomatic service. With UN sponsorship, he worked with the German government to convene a meeting in Bonn, Germany, from November 27 to December 5, 2001.

Among those in attendance were representatives of the four major anti-Taliban groups: the Northern Alliance; a group of exiles with ties to Iran; a group loyal to Afghanistan's former king, Mohammad Zahir Shah, who had been living in exile in Rome for many years; and a group of Pashtun exiles based in Pakistan. Four of the representatives to the conference were women, notable for the fact that women had traditionally played no role in Afghan politics. The Taliban were deliberately excluded from attending, despite Pakistan's lobbying for their inclusion. Representatives from the United States and several other countries were also in attendance.

The Bonn Conference laid out a plan for a peaceful political transition in Afghanistan. On December 5, negotiations among the principals concluded with the drafting of the Agreement on Provisional Arrangements in Afghanistan Pending the Re-establishment of Permanent Government Institutions. This agreement called for an emergency Loya Jirga (Great Assembly) in six months, at which the Transitional Authority, a temporary

The Bonn Conference in December 2001 laid out a plan for a peaceful transition of power in Afghanistan, which would include free elections.

government, would be established to govern the country until a permanent representative government was created.

A constitutional Loya Jirga to adopt a new constitution was required by the agreement to take place within eighteen months of the establishment of the Transitional Authority. It would outline the basic structure of the administration, delegate powers to handle the affairs of state, and lay the groundwork for the creation of a central bank.

Hamid Karzai was chosen as chair of the interim adminis-tration. There was strong support for Karzai in the United States. He had good connections across the non-Taliban Afghan spectrum, and he was the best choice among all the candidates to create and maintain a broad governing coalition. Negotiators had worked hard to achieve ethnic balance in the makeup of the interim administration, a theme that Karzai also attempted to follow throughout his leadership.

The Internal Security Assistance Force

The Bonn Conference also called for the creation of an Interna-tional Security Assistance Force (ISAF), which was established by the UN on December 20, 2001. The ISAF's mandate was to secure the capital of Kabul with a force of about five thousand soldiers from eighteen countries. The UK provided the largest contingent, followed by France and Germany. Other nations provided smaller groups or equipment and medical services. Leadership was meant to operate on a six-month rotating basis among the nations, but control was permanently shifted to NATO in August 2003. NATO pushed to expand the ISAF man-date in December, and additional ISAF forces began to move out beyond Kabul to secure and pacify other areas.

The United States was reluctant to pledge troops to the ISAF initially because military leaders did not want American forces in-volved in peacekeeping. Undersecretary of defense for policy Dou-glas Feith explains the American position: "We couldn't put U.S. forces in ISAF because other countries might conclude that the United States would bail them out if they got into trouble. The State Department answer . . . was to expand the ISAF. We wanted to allow the Afghans to establish their own security."[32] Operation Enduring Freedom continued independent combat operations in the regions outside Kabul, but after NATO took command, the United States contributed heavily to the ISAF while conducting its own operations.

The Security Dilemma

The establishment of the Afghan Transitional Authority along with a concrete plan for developing a constitution and a permanent government to be elected by the people was a major step forward in the rebuilding of Afghanistan, but it was merely the beginning. The issue of maintaining security still loomed large over the entire process.

As early as March 2002, al Qaeda fighters had regrouped in the Shah-i-Kot Valley in Paktia Province near the Pakistani border south of Kabul. The Taliban also began rebuilding their militia in Paktia Province, which they used as a base to begin launching guerrilla attacks against U.S. forces. Many of these attacks were hit-and-run strikes, in which small bands of Taliban and al Qaeda fighters would open fire on U.S. troops, then retreat into the mountains to wait out the response.

Taliban and al Qaeda fighters moved freely back and forth across the Pakistani border, taking refuge in the Federally Administered Tribal Areas (FATA). The FATA is a region in northwestern Pakistan along the Afghan border that consists of several, mainly Pashtun, tribal groups that live with considerable freedom from the Pakistani government. Taliban fighters were able to mix in with the local population and gain considerable influence in the region. They quickly established a base of operations to plan their military campaign.

U.S. forces initially believed that there were only a couple hundred fighters, but in reality there were well over one thousand and maybe as many as five thousand. U.S. forces engaged in a number of military operations throughout 2002 and 2003 to eliminate the threat posed by the Taliban and al Qaeda fighters. They inflicted a large number of casualties, but they were ultimately unsuccessful in stopping the insurgents, who gathered reinforcements as their exploits became known to Islamic fundamentalists who supported their cause.

The Taliban and al Qaeda operated separately, but their tactics and goals were the same—engage U.S. forces in small battles that harassed the American positions and reminded the population that the Taliban and al Qaeda were still a force to be reckoned with. They also attacked civilians in towns and rural areas and killed or kidnapped international humanitarian workers attempting to aid the population.

Afghan soldiers man a position on the Pakistani border in 2004 in an effort to prevent Taliban and al Qaeda forces from crossing the border.

William Maley, author of *Rescuing Afghanistan*, explains the effectiveness of these actions. "Attacks on aid workers, travelers, ethnic minorities, and school teachers are politically potent not because the victims are politically important, but because the very fact that the attack occurs symbolizes the inability of the central state to discharge a core function, namely to protect civilians from attacks of this sort."[33]

HUMANITARIAN AID MUST BE COORDINATED WITH MILITARY STRATEGY

"Without unity of command throughout civilian and military organizations, there cannot be the unity of effort needed to support Afghanistan in defeating a ruthless insurgency."—Lt. Joshua W. Welle, U.S. Navy officer

Joshua W. Welle. "Civil-Military Integration in Afghanistan." *Joint Force Quarterly*, no. 56, 2010, p. 54.

U.S. and allied policy planners recognized that Afghans were going to have to share the burden of security in the short term and fully take over security responsibilities in the long term if the country were to remain stable. The creation of the Afghan National Army (ANA) was necessary in order to avoid a large, long-term foreign military presence in the country. This project was heavily funded and administered by the United States as part of a so-called build-up, stand-down strategy. This strategy is defined as building up the Afghan forces so that U.S. forces could eventually disengage. The more Afghan troops that were in the field, the fewer American troops that would be needed.

Training Afghans to become part of a stable military force was a difficult process. The Afghans were not used to the formal training and disciplinary methods of the U.S. and allied forces, and many of them tired easily of the hard work that was involved. This led to high desertion rates among trainees. Many trainees also harbored a mercenary mentality that motivated them to focus only on the short-term benefits of obtaining weapons and the pay that came with training, even though the pay was rather low. Their allegiances were often to their own tribes or villages, not the country at large. Low literacy rates among the Afghans also hindered their training, and education in complex strategic methods was frequently impossible.

U.S. forces faced similar obstacles in developing the Afghan National Police (ANP). Afghanistan had existed for so many

Doctors Without Borders: Bringing Aid to a War Zone

Doctors Without Borders is an international medical humanitarian organization created by doctors and journalists in France in 1971, also known as Médecins sans Frontières (MSF). MSF provides aid in close to sixty countries to people threatened by armed conflict, natural disaster, disease, and malnutrition.

MSF withdrew from Afghanistan in 2004 after five staff members were killed in an ambush. The Taliban claimed responsibility for the attack, stating that humanitarian aid workers were targets for the insurgents because they were tied to American and other Western interests. The organization returned in 2009 to continue its work among Afghan civilians. Doctors Without Borders described the return process in an annual report:

> It was crucial for MSF to secure agreements with all parties to ensure the hospitals were safe environments, so a 'no weapons allowed' policy was successfully implemented.

> In the district hospital in the East of Kabul, MSF worked to improve treatment procedures, the emergency room, and maternity services. By the end of the year, nearly 19,000 consultations and 1,000 deliveries had been carried out, and almost 9,900 people had been immunized through the Extended Immunization program. . . .

> MSF also started to support Boost provincial hospital in Lashkargah, the capital of Helmand province. Lashkargah's inhabitants have been severely affected by the conflict, and this 150-bed facility is one of only two general

years without basic rule of law that it was difficult to instill concepts such as gathering evidence in criminal cases or respecting the rights of the accused. Trainees were often illiterate and could not process police paperwork or argue cases before judges and attorneys. It was also difficult to find recruits who did not have criminal records or prior associations with the Taliban, warlords, or drug gangs. Pay for police recruits and officers was low compared with what could be earned in illegal activities like

care public hospitals in south Afghanistan. MSF extended its support to all health services in the hospital, including maternity, pediatrics, surgery and emergency rooms. Since the start of the project, 1,100 consultations, more than 60 surgical interventions and nearly 160 deliveries have taken place.

Doctors Without Borders. "International Activity Report 2009." www.doctorswithoutborders.org/publications/ar/report .cfm?id=4482&cat=activity-report&ref=tag-index.

A Doctors Without Borders physician attends an Afghan woman in 2003. The organization was forced to leave Afghanistan after the Taliban killed five staff members.

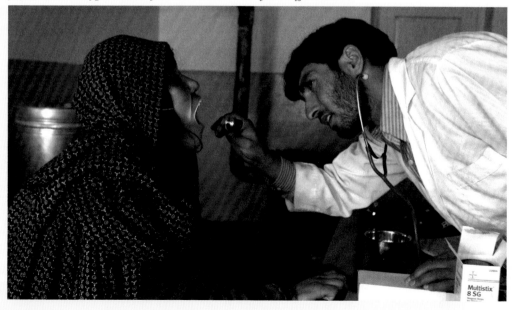

Afghanistan's flourishing drug trade or the black market. Some police officers operated mainly as gangsters in uniforms, and citizens found it hard to distinguish their behavior from that of the warlords and Taliban leaders who had plagued them previously. There was also a lack of decent equipment like guns, body armor, uniforms, and other tools of law enforcement.

The absence of a cohesive national police force and an Afghan army led the United States to continue its reliance on warlords. The warlords had been part of the original coalition to topple the Taliban, but now they had become an integral part of the U.S. strategy to secure the country and muster support for Karzai's government. Some U.S. policy planners assumed that since the warlords were anti-Taliban, they would essentially be pro-America. This was not the case. Subodh Atal writes, "Many of the warlords have survived for decades through a combination of aid from external forces, their own ruthlessness, and a lucrative role in drug smuggling. The loyalties of these warlords are accordingly fickle, and they have little interest in supporting a strong central government that would encroach on their power."[34]

Karzai was likewise dependent on the warlords to prop up his government. His tendency was to move warlords to other areas of operation to diffuse their power rather than remove them entirely from the government. One Afghan provisional governor noted, "Keeping warlords in power is weakening the government. The more the government pays them off, the stronger they will become and the weaker the government will be."[35]

A Country in Need

Living conditions in Afghanistan had deteriorated greatly during the Soviet war, but the medieval rule of the Taliban made Afghans' suffering even worse. Under Taliban rule, international humanitarian efforts were hampered by the regime's complete rejection of modern influences. Organizations like Doctors Without Borders and the International Red Cross were often barred from entering the country, and aid workers faced the threat of jail time or even murder at the hands of strict Taliban leaders. It was not until the Taliban were overthrown that the true extent of the humanitarian disaster in Afghanistan became known.

At the end of 2001, Afghanistan ranked at or near the bottom of the world in every major social indicator. The infant mortality rate was 150 per 1,000 live births. By comparison, the infant mortality rate in the United States at this time was 7 per 1,000 live births. Life expectancy in Afghanistan was approximately forty-four years. In the United States, it was seventy-seven. Afghans suffered a 50 percent rate of malnutrition, and fewer than 10 percent of rural households could report a health-care facility of some sort in their village. Only 28 percent of the population was literate.

CIVIL AND MILITARY AID EFFORTS NEED TO BE SEPARATE

"Aid used as a tool in the counterinsurgency strategy continues to endanger aid workers and undermine sustainable development."
—Lynn Yoshikawa and Dawn Calabia, activists with Refugees International

Lynn Yoshikawa and Dawn Calabia. "Afghanistan: In a Time of Conflict." Refugees International, December 1, 2010. www.refugeesinternational.org/policy/field-report/afghanistan-time-conflict.

Food sources were hard to come by because farmland had been improperly managed, leaving the soil devoid of nutrients necessary to grow crops. Besides, much of the available farmland was devoted to growing opium poppies for the profitable heroin trade. When there was adequate farmland, freshwater was scarce. Electricity was also nonexistent in many villages.

There was no real market economy in the country. Afghanistan had no industrial capacity or commercial sector to speak of, so there was no source of steady employment for the citizens. The only opportunities for many men to make money and provide for their families was to work for warlords or corrupt politicians as hired thugs in a variety of black-market enterprises, chief among them being the narcotics business.

The Drug Trade

The only element of the Afghan economy that thrived was linked to the drug trade. Afghanistan is the world's largest grower of opium poppies, the plant used to make opium, from which heroin is created. Opium production increased rapidly after the Taliban were removed from power, reaching an all-time high in 2006. According to U.S. Drug Enforcement Administration statistics, "Opium production in Afghanistan rose from an estimated 1,278 metric tons of potential oven-dried opium produced in 2002 to 2,865 metric tons in 2003, and to 4,950 metric tons in 2004. . . . In 2005, although opium production declined to an estimated 4,475 metric tons, Afghanistan remained the source of approximately 92 percent of the global illicit opium supply."[36] The growth, cultivation, sale, and distribution of opium amounted to 60 percent of Afghanistan's gross domestic product in 2006 and involved some 2 million Afghans from virtually every level of society. Farmers and their families, corrupt police, ANA soldiers, politicians, and warlords all had a stake in the drug trade. There is still a great deal of activity in the south. For instance, poppies are virtually the only crop grown in Helmand Province.

The importance of opium production in Afghanistan complicates the solutions for stabilizing the country. The U.S. State Department noted in its 2009 "International Narcotics Control Strategy Report" that "Afghanistan's narcotics industry continues to threaten efforts to establish security, governance, and a licit economy throughout the country."[37] This sentiment has been used by policy planners calling for the eradication (destruction) of poppy fields across Afghanistan along with the arrest of anyone involved in poppy cultivation and production.

Eradication cannot be easily accomplished. Aerial spraying is largely ineffective because the fields are spread out over wide areas. Also, the eradication of some poppy fields will only make the surviving crop that much more valuable, raising its price and ultimately attracting more people to become involved in its production. The UN Office on Drugs and Crime noted in 2008 that farmers with the highest incomes often live in provinces

An armed member of the Afghan Public Protection Force destroys a poppy field in Helmand Province. Despite eradication efforts, Afghanistan still supplies 92 percent of the world's illicit opium.

Afghanistan's First Presidential Election

Post-Taliban Afghanistan held its first presidential election on October 9, 2004, as directed by the agreement reached at the Bonn Conference. *New York Times* columnist William Safire captures the importance of the event:

> Against all dire predictions and threats from terrorists, Afghanistan —breeding ground of Al Qaeda under the medieval rule of Taliban fundamentalists—has just held the first presidential election in its bloodstained history.
>
> The winner was Hamid Karzai, 46, a politician of the majority Pashtuns, who emerged with 55 percent of the eight million votes cast.
>
> A bigger winner was the Afghan people. Their men . . . had fallen victim to regional dissension and Taliban fanatics supported by Arab terrorists. Their women were hidden at home and treated like slaves. Now, thanks to the U.S.-led intervention and their own willingness to fight for freedom, Afghans lined up to vote in the first presidential election in that nation's history.
>
> The biggest winner of this unfettering event is the cause of democracy in the world, and especially in this region, which much of the West assumed was too culturally backward to express a longing for freedom.

William Safire. "The Best Political News of 2004." *New York Times*, October 27, 2004. www.nytimes.com/2004/10/27/opinion/27safire.html?scp=44&sq=Afghanistan+elections+2004&st=nyt.

Afghan women line up to vote in Afghanistan's first presidential election. Under the Taliban, women had been forbidden to vote.

with the highest opium production. For many of these farmers, involvement in opium cultivation means the difference between supporting their families and complete poverty. Calls for the arrest of anyone involved in production would lead to otherwise law-abiding Afghan citizens going to jail, and this would cause resentment of the U.S. presence by a larger portion of the population. Maley suggests that a long-term solution to the drug problem "will be found not in crude eradication or even 'crop substitution' but in fostering alternative livelihoods. . . . It is necessary to rebuild broader institutions of governance and finance so that incentives begin to change."[38]

America's Deadly Distraction

America's pursuit of terrorists and the states that support them was not confined to Afghanistan. In 2002 the Bush administration made the case to the international community that Iraqi dictator Saddam Hussein was working to develop weapons of mass destruction that could be used against the United States and its allies. Due to concerns about such weapons and other grievances with Saddam, the United States on March 19, 2003, led a multinational invasion of Iraq, beginning a lengthy war there.

The situation in Afghanistan in 2002 was far from settled and much work remained to stabilize the country. Taliban and al Qaeda fighters were at this point emerging from hideouts across the border in Pakistan, and U.S. and coalition forces were caught in an increasing number of engagements with the enemy. Just the same, U.S. military planners turned their focus to the removal of Saddam from power, and they began a military buildup to accomplish this goal.

"From day one it was Iraq, Iraq, Iraq," recalls former U.S. deputy secretary of state Richard Armitage. "Afghanistan was really an accidental war for much of the Administration. . . . And once it became clear the Taliban was likely to fall, senior Pentagon officials wanted to turn to Iraq as quickly as possible."[39]

The invasion of Iraq came at the expense of the American military commitment in Afghanistan. Equipment that could have helped U.S. soldiers beat back the resurgence of the Taliban and al Qaeda was pledged to the Iraqi invasion. Similarly, plans for deploying more U.S. troops to Afghanistan were scrapped in favor of sending them to Iraq.

By the time the United States and its allies removed Saddam from power in the spring of 2003, the situation in Afghanistan had become more desperate. American forces there had to make do with whatever resources happened to be available to combat the problem, which grew rapidly beyond their ability to handle. Maley notes that "the invasion of Iraq in March 2003 created an additional obstacle to Afghanistan receiving the continued attention it deserves."[40]

FIGHTING THE INSURGENCY

The security situation in Afghanistan continued to deteriorate in late 2002 and early 2003. After managing to evade U.S. forces throughout mid-2002, the remnants of the Taliban prepared to launch the insurgency that Mullah Mohammed Omar had promised in late 2001. Taliban forces began to actively recruit fighters in both Afghanistan and Pakistan to launch a holy war against the Afghan government and the U.S.-led coalition. Many of the recruits came from madrassas in the tribal areas of Pakistan, much like the radical Islamic fighters who had supported the Taliban in the mid-1990s.

Al Qaeda and Taliban leaders built training camps along the Pakistani border to train recruits in guerrilla tactics. During the winter of 2002–2003, the Taliban reorganized and reconstituted their forces in preparation for a major offensive that would take place when warmer weather arrived. They gathered in groups of about fifty fighters and focused their attacks on remote U.S. and Afghan outposts. They engaged in hit-and-run attacks on Afghan convoys and then broke up into small squads of five to ten fighters to easily evade the pursuing allied forces. U.S. officials questioned the ability and the willingness of the Pakistani military to secure the border and prevent the flow of the fighters into Afghanistan.

The Al Qaeda–trained insurgents also built and deployed improvised explosive devices (IEDs). These homemade bombs began appearing along roads traveled by U.S. forces and in urban areas. They were hard to spot and could be detonated remotely or triggered like land mines when they came into contact with vehicles or individual soldiers. Troop transports and other military vehicles not already reinforced with armor were often

The remains of a U.S. Army vehicle show the damage from a roadside explosion caused by an improvised explosive device, or IED. Two soldiers were killed in the explosion and three were wounded.

completely destroyed in these attacks. U.S. and allied soldiers suffered more casualties from IEDs than they did in battle. The insurgents also raided the fledgling Afghan police force precinct stations, using rocket attacks and suicide bombers.

In the midst of the growing insurgency, in late 2004 Osama bin Laden resurfaced from the mountainous regions of Pakistan, boosting recruitment and morale for the al Qaeda fighters in the field.

Afghan citizens, who once again found themselves in the midst of civil conflict, questioned the effectiveness and sustainability of Karzai's government. U.S. and ISAF policy planners also began to question Karzai's ability to control the situation when it became apparent that corruption was running rampant among his senior staff.

The Troubled Afghan Government

It could not be denied by U.S. officials that Karzai presided over a weak central government in Kabul. He was surrounded by a staff that was not fully competent. Many members of his government were not even loyal to him or the country as a whole. They had their own agendas, whether lining their own pockets through the drug trade or secretly supporting the Taliban.

Karzai has often attempted to pacify potential rivals by giving them positions in the government. This has caused bad feelings with legitimate members of his government because it sends the message that bad behavior will be rewarded while competence and loyalty are no longer important for advancement. Kim Barker, South Asia correspondent for the *Chicago Tribune*, notes, "The real worry is that [Karzai's] made all these promises to these power brokers and that he's going to put in people who aren't necessarily qualified for each job."[41] There is also a concern about exactly what promises have been made to various warlords.

Karzai's political management style was always based on networking, the construction of alliances, and patronage (the granting of government jobs). Observers note that Karzai had a significant weakness that was not apparent when he first came to power: his lack of understanding or appreciation for detailed policy making. This became evident when the constitution that was adopted established a strong presidency with the power to dictate policy, a power he did not handle well.

Karzai's method of patronage proved harmful to public perceptions of his administration. The people assigned to various posts did not have a vested interest in the successful accomplishment of their duties. Furthermore, Afghan citizens came to believe their government was becoming a dictatorship and not a democracy because a growing number of elected officials were more focused on personal enrichment than the will of the voters.

PRIVATE CONTRACTORS ARE NECESSARY IN AFGHANISTAN

"Because we often need to mobilize or demobilize quickly, contractors allow us to meet mission requirements rapidly and flexibly. Further, contractors enable us to rapidly hire large numbers of former police officers with recent law enforcement experience."
—David T. Johnson, assistant secretary, Bureau of International Narcotics and Law Enforcement

David T. Johnson. "Use of Contractors to Train Afghan National Police." U.S. Department of State, December 18, 2009. www.state.gov/p/inl/rls/rm/133872.htm.

Ahmad Wali Karzai, the president's brother and a prominent political figure in Kandahar Province, has been accused on numerous occasions of profiting from the Afghan drug trade and other illegal activities. Counternarcotics officials, ISAF commanders, and NATO officials have all called upon President Karzai to rein in his brother. An October 27, 2009, *New York Times* story reported that Ahmad Wali had been a paid asset of the CIA for eight years, brokering secret meetings with Taliban leaders and helping the CIA operate a civilian-run military strike force that targets insurgents. Both the CIA and the Karzai brothers denied the allegations that Ahmad Wali was involved with the CIA or the drug trade. President Karzai told

Time magazine in 2008, "My brother can . . . easily be accused [so as] to put pressure on me. . . . Allegations have been there, but never have they come to me with proof."[42] The accusations against Ahmad Wali, which came as no surprise to the Afghan people, were symbolic of how prevalent corruption became in the government.

Sirajuddin Haqqani: Leader of the Haqqani Network

Sirajuddin Haqqani, a Pashtun warlord based in Pakistan, leads the Haqqani Network, one of the most powerful groups of the Afghan insurgency. His forces have committed a number of atrocities, including the bombing of an Afghan school in 2008 that killed several schoolchildren. Haqqani's actions earned a $5 million reward for his capture from the United States in 2009, as noted on the State Department website:

> The U.S. Department of State has authorized a reward of up to $5 million for information leading to the location, arrest, and/or conviction of Sirajuddin Haqqani (aka Siraj Haqqani).

> Sirajuddin Haqqani, a senior leader of the Haqqani terrorist network founded by his father Jalaladin Haqqani, maintains close ties to al-Qa'ida. During an interview with an American news organization, Haqqani admitted

planning the January 14, 2008 attack against the Serena Hotel in Kabul that killed six people, including American citizen Thor David Hesla.

Haqqani also admitted to having planned the April 2008 assassination attempt on Afghan President Hamid Karzai. He has coordinated and participated in cross-border attacks against U.S. and Coalition forces in Afghanistan. He is believed to be located in the Federally Administered Tribal Areas of Pakistan.

We encourage anyone with information on Haqqani's location to contact the nearest U.S. embassy or consulate, any U.S. military commander, or the Rewards for Justice staff.

U.S. Department of State. "Rewards for Justice: Sirajuddin Haqqani." 2009. www.state.gov/r/pa/prs/ps/2009/03/120864.htm.

Afghan president Hamid Karzai's political management style is based on networking, alliance construction, and patronage, but critics say he lacks understanding of detailed policy making and is corrupt.

Karzai's inability to combat corruption and meet the desires of his people for peace and economic development has led to strained relations with the United States. In 2009, secretary of state Hillary Clinton asserted, "We are not going to be providing any civilian aid to Afghanistan unless we have a certification that, if it goes into the Afghan Government in any form, that we are going to have ministries that we can hold accountable."[43]

Causes of the Insurgency

According to terrorism expert and author Seth G. Jones, Karzai's government was not weakened by the insurgency, as some U.S. officials believed. In testimony before the House Foreign Affairs Committee in 2009, Jones asserted, rather, that Karzai's ineffective government was to blame for the growing crisis. "Security challenges don't stem from a strong insurgency, but rather from a weak and increasingly unpopular government,"[44] he noted.

The instability of Karzai's government certainly provided a powerful recruiting tool for the insurgency, which reached its peak strength in 2007 and 2008. Many Afghan people found that the opportunities for a safer country and a better life that had been promised by the new government were not being met. Lack of faith in state institutions drew many to the insurgency.

These new recruits were not all sympathetic to the Taliban, which was only one faction in the insurgency. There were other groups, including al Qaeda, the Pakistani-supported Haqqani Network, and Gulbuddin Hekmatyar's Hezb-i-Islami, which reemerged in 2008. There were also drug smugglers, local tribes, warlords, and even government officials and security forces looking to increase their own power in the country. They all had different agendas, but they were united by a common hatred of U.S. and ISAF forces. They despised Karzai's government and viewed him as a puppet of the Americans, even after he began to fall out of favor with the U.S. government.

The insurgency relied on a strategy often referred to as "death by a thousand cuts." This strategy recognized the fact that the insurgents did not have the military strength to fight the U.S. and its allies head on. Instead, it relied on a continuous series of small attacks on U.S. forces and Afghan institutions. Suicide bombings, assassinations, sabotage, and propaganda were all tools used in this effort. The goal of the insurgents was to inflict casualties on U.S. forces without allowing the United States to make any sustained progress against them. Then the American public would come to believe that victory was impossible and force their government to withdraw from Afghanistan. George Crile writes, "Special Forces doctrine held that if a guerilla insurgency survives and grows, then it is by definition winning."[45] All the insurgents had to do was not lose.

The Battle for Stability

The Taliban's fight against U.S. and Afghan forces in the south and east of Afghanistan brought supporters to their cause. The Taliban offered a level of stability that the Afghan government had not provided. Kenneth Katzman, a specialist in Middle Eastern affairs at the Congressional Research Service, writes, "Many Afghans are said to have turned to the Taliban as a source of impartial and rapid justice, in contrast to the slow and corrupt processes instituted by the central government."[46]

Throughout 2004 and 2005, the Taliban had executed military attacks on Afghan and American forces and then expanded to terrorist attacks on civilians in major cities. Despite several counterattacks and raids on Taliban positions, the U.S. military was not able to lock down the insurgents. In 2006 a deployment of roughly eight thousand ISAF soldiers moved in, relieving a large portion of the U.S. detachment. Operation Enduring Freedom shifted its focus to the east along the Afghanistan/Pakistan border, where U.S. commanders believed a large number of infiltrations were taking place.

In 2004 and 2005, the ISAF was successful in establishing control over military operations in the north and west. After 2006, much of the combat activity took place in the south and east where the Taliban were believed to have ten thousand fighters. U.S. and ISAF troops launched a large, coordinated strike in 2007 in order to stop an anticipated Taliban spring offensive. Several battles raged throughout the year, and allied military commanders called for more troops. By the end of 2008, the United States had a total of thirty-nine thousand soldiers in Afghanistan, twenty-three thousand of whom were pledged to the ISAF, which had a total strength of over fifty-five thousand.

The significantly larger allied force was not able to completely halt the insurgent attacks, which grew bolder and more frequent. In June Taliban fighters broke twelve hundred prisoners out of a

A Taliban Jailbreak

On June 14, 2008, insurgents in Afghanistan executed a daring jailbreak in Kandahar that demonstrated how effective and dangerous they had become. Carlotta Gall describes the event in the *New York Times*:

> In a brazen attack, Taliban fighters assaulted the main prison in the southern Afghan city of Kandahar on Friday night, blowing up the mud walls, killing 15 guards and freeing around 1,200 inmates. Among the escapees were about 350 Taliban members, including commanders, would-be suicide bombers and assassins, said Ahmed Wali Karzai, the head of Kandahar's provincial council and a brother of President Hamid Karzai.
>
> "It is very dangerous for security. They are the most experienced killers and they all managed to escape," he said by telephone from Kandahar.
>
> A Taliban spokesman, Qari Yousuf Ahmadi, said that the attack was carried out by 30 insurgents on motorbikes and two suicide bombers, and that they had freed about 400 Taliban members, The Associated Press reported.
>
> The breakout from Sarposa Prison will present enormous security challenges for Afghan and NATO forces surrounding Kandahar, President Karzai's home city but also the spiritual capital of the Taliban.

Carlotta Gall. "Taliban Free 1,200 Inmates in Attack on Afghan Prison." *New York Times*, June 14, 2008. www.nytimes.com/2008/06/14/world/asia/14kandahar.html.

An Afghan policeman looks through the debris of the Kandahar prison, where explosions killed fifteen people and allowed the escape of twelve hundred prisoners, of which about a third were Taliban.

jail in Kandahar, which was under ISAF control, and in July they launched an attack on an ISAF outpost. The military victories achieved by U.S. and ISAF soldiers were brief, and they were not able to hold territory for long periods. Even with more troops, the situation was not improving.

The Counterinsurgency Strategy

Many policy planners had argued from the early days of America's involvement in Afghanistan that a smaller U.S. presence in the country would prevent the perception of the U.S. as an occupier rather than a liberator. This is often referred to as a "light footprint" strategy, and it relied on a smaller American force working closely with the Afghan government to build up its institutions and become self-reliant. Unfortunately, as the insurgency gathered momentum, military strategists observed that the light footprint strategy may have actually hampered the ability of the United States to beat back the insurgency in its early months. Gary Schmitt, director of the Program on Advanced Strategic Studies at the American Enterprise Institute, writes, "From 2001 until [2010], both the United States and its allies have taken an economy of force approach. There were enough troops to topple the Taliban and then just enough to keep Afghanistan from reverting to Taliban control. There have never been enough forces, however, to defeat them and stabilize the country."[47]

Seth G. Jones writes that the U.S. presence in Afghanistan needs to focus on three distinct tasks in order to combat the insurgency successfully. First, corruption has to be addressed and rooted out. The United States and other nations need to encourage Afghan leaders to draft tough laws and arrest and prosecute corrupt officials. It is somewhat tolerable for the population to view the Afghan government as weak, he states, but they have to at least see it as legitimate.

Second, according to Jones, U.S. forces have to focus more of their resources on supporting local and provincial governments. The Americans should support legitimate tribal leaders and cooperative locals with financial and material rewards, as well as provide them with aid and security, since they would most likely be the target of insurgent attacks and criminal networks. If these local leaders receive the protection of U.S. forces, they would be more likely to trust the American presence and ultimately support U.S. and Afghan government efforts, Jones contends.

CONTRACTORS ENDANGER THE MISSION IN AFGHANISTAN

"The barrage of rounds [in a private contractor counterattack on Taliban forces in 2010] was shot so indiscriminately—U.S. soldiers derisively referred to it as the 'spray and pray' method—that they were just as likely to hit innocent civilians, or their own men, as they were the Taliban. If this kind of undisciplined response were the exception, U.S. and NATO commanders might not be so concerned. But it is such a regular occurrence."—Kevin Sites, a solo journalist who has filed reports with CNN, Yahoo.com, the GlobalPost, and other news sources

Kevin Sites. "Afghanistan: Private Insecurity." GlobalPost, August 11, 2010. www.global post.com/dispatch/afghanistan/100810/private-insecurity.

A third component in the strategy outlined by Jones calls for eliminating the safe haven over the border in the FATA of Pakistan. He writes, "It is imperative that the United States persuade Pakistani military and civilian leaders to conduct a sustained campaign against militants mounting attacks in Afghanistan."[48] The United States had received the Pakistani government's cooperation with the invasion and the arrest of several key al Qaeda operatives. But Pakistan had also proved that it could not be relied upon to support the U.S. counterinsurgency or the Afghan government.

Pakistan: An Uncertain Ally

Prior to the September 11, 2001, terrorist attacks on the United States, Pakistan was considered a volatile state by Western nations because of the growing strength of radical Islamic groups within its borders. It was also a nuclear power, and the U.S. government feared that a nuclear warhead could end up in the hands of al Qaeda. General Pervez Musharraf, the military dictator of Pakistan when the United States first invaded Afghanistan, came to power in a 1998 coup and later made himself president. He had attempted to control the radical groups, but his efforts had been largely ineffective because of the strong support they received from the ISI and other elements within the Pakistani government.

When U.S. military planners approached Musharraf in 2001 with the request to aid their efforts in Afghanistan, they made it

Pakistani general Pervez Musharraf became president of the country after a 1998 military coup. Musharraf walked a fine line between supporting the Americans and appeasing the radical Islamic elements in Pakistan.

clear that they expected his support. Fearing that the United States might actually attack Pakistan as well as Afghanistan, Musharraf tried to straddle the fine line between supporting the Americans and appeasing the radical elements in his own country.

Musharraf allowed U.S. forces to use Pakistani airfields for the 2001 invasion, and his government froze the bank accounts of Islamist organizations linked to al Qaeda. In return, the United States lifted sanctions it had placed on Pakistan for its pursuit and development of nuclear weapons. The United States also restructured Pakistan's $400 million debt and influenced the World Bank and the International Monetary Fund to do the same. Bush publicly praised Musharraf for his efforts.

Continued Pakistani support for the U.S. war against terrorism led to the capture of Khalid Sheikh Mohammed, the architect of the September 11 attacks. Al Qaeda members Abu Zubaydah and Ahmed Ghailani, a planner of the 1998 embassy bombings, were also captured with Pakistani help. This in part led to the *9/11 Commission Report*'s conclusion that Pakistan was becoming a reliable ally.

Retired army general Barry McCaffrey, after a 2007 trip to Pakistan to meet with top officials, stated, "The Pakistanis are not actively supporting the Taliban—nor do they have a strategic purpose to destabilize Afghanistan."[49] Evidence demonstrated, however, that this was not the case. Musharraf's attempts to control radical elements in the madrassahs were not consistent. Individuals within the ISI actively supported Taliban elements in Pakistan. They provided sanctuary to insurgents who later crossed the border and attacked U.S. forces. They sent money and logistical support to insurgents in Afghanistan, and they were in contact with Mullah Omar and members of the Haqqani Network.

The issue of border security was also a problem. Eight years of air strikes, military patrols, and added checkpoints had had little effect in keeping insurgents based in Pakistan from infiltrating Afghanistan. Musharraf's government had engaged in a number of agreements in 2006 with tribal leaders in the FATA, including those allied with the Taliban. After this point, Pakistan did little to patrol or enforce the border in that region. In

September 2008 U.S. special forces landed in Pakistan for the first time and attacked al Qaeda positions. The Pakistani government was outraged and refused to allow U.S. or ISAF forces to operate in Pakistan.

Pakistan's unwillingness to cooperate with securing the Afghan border frustrated the United States, as this 2010 State Department cable states: "The borders are porous. Taliban and militant extremists are constantly crossing the border with Afghanistan and engaging in terrorist and smuggling activity. The rugged terrain makes it difficult to patrol and control the border."[50]

The stability of Pakistan itself came into question in 2007 when Musharraf's power base began to crumble. He faced growing opposition from people who wanted democratic reforms, but he also faced a growing militant threat from Islamic fundamentalists who were angered by his ties to the United States. Violence broke out in the capital city of Islamabad and other cities, and the economy was shaken. Musharraf declared a national emergency on November 3 and fired the entire Pakistani Supreme Court. He later reinstalled them after major protests.

Impeachment proceedings were brought against Musharraf for abuses of power and violating the constitution. He resigned on August 18, 2008, rather than face trial. His successor, Asif Ali Zardari, won the presidential election in a landslide. Relations with Afghanistan improved almost immediately, with Karzai attending Zardari's inauguration on September 9. The two leaders pledged cooperation in fighting terrorism, but Zardari's relations with the United States remained tense.

U.S. president Barack Obama, who succeeded Bush in 2009, sought to establish better relations with both Pakistan and Afghanistan, but his efforts were not met with full support from Pakistan. A February 2011 Congressional Research Service review noted that Pakistan made political deals with a number of groups in Afghanistan, "protecting certain Afghan militant factions . . . that might play a role in a post-settlement Afghanistan."[51] Elements of the Pakistani government that have aided extremists sought to place Pakistan in a position from which it would be able to influence Afghanistan's future. They

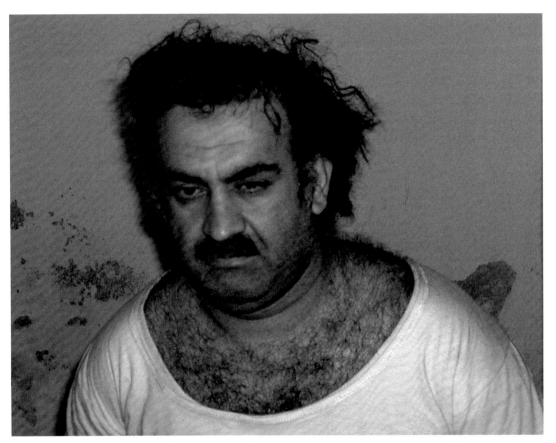

Pakistani support for the U.S. battle against terrorism led to the capture of the architect of the 9/11 attacks, Khalid Sheikh Mohammed.

believed that the United States would eventually withdraw from the region, and their support of the insurgency indicated that they wanted to hasten that withdrawal.

Pakistan's history of support for the Taliban, which included providing them with weapons, ammunition, fuel, training, and intelligence, made it an unreliable partner in rebuilding Afghanistan. The United States could not ignore Pakistan in its strategy to pacify Afghanistan. Nor could it ignore the continued economic and social instability within Pakistan. Stephen Biddle, senior fellow for defense policy at the Council on Foreign Relations, explains, "We're afraid that failure in Afghanistan will enable

After Pervez Musharraf was charged with abuse of power, he resigned. Asif Ali Zardari won the subsequent presidential election by a landslide.

al-Qaeda, strengthen it, create bases for it, and especially make it more likely that al-Qaeda and its allies could topple the government of Pakistan and get access to Pakistan's nuclear weapons. That's all one or two steps removed from roadside bombings and ambushes on the road between Kabul and Kandahar."[52]

RETHINKING AMERICA'S COMMITMENT

Domestic criticism of the U.S. commitment in Afghanistan grew steadily in 2007 and 2008 when it became apparent that the U.S. and coalition forces had made no significant gains in stabilizing the Afghan government or in containing the insurgency. Many members of the ISAF had tired of the conflict and were looking either to reduce their presence or leave Afghanistan. Furthermore, critics of American involvement believed that the mission in Afghanistan had grown far beyond the war's original goals. What had started out as an attempt to defeat al Qaeda had transformed over several years into a larger mission to create a stable government, fight the drug trade, and provide broad economic assistance to the country. Innocent and Carpenter point out, "The longer we stay and the more money we spend, the more we'll feel compelled to remain in the country to validate the investment."[53]

U.S. and allied forces were victorious in a number of engagements with the enemy in 2007 and 2008, but the insurgency continued unabated. Additionally, several coalition members began drawing down the number of troops they kept in Afghanistan or, in some cases, pulling out altogether. This placed a greater burden on U.S. and British forces to continue the fight. Many nations remained committed to aid in the rebuilding of Afghanistan, but most did not want to engage in military operations. Some nations were expressly forbidden to do so by their own laws and constitutions.

Upon taking office, President Obama pledged to renew America's commitment in Afghanistan, and over time set out a plan to increase the U.S. presence there.

When General Stanley McChrystal took control of U.S. operations in Afghanistan, he said that a significant troop buildup was necessary to gain the upper hand over the insurgency.

The American Military Buildup

General Stanley McChrystal, commander of the special operations forces that had succeeded in neutralizing the Iraq insurgency, took control of U.S. operations in Afghanistan on June 10, 2009. He immediately recognized that a significant troop buildup was necessary to gain the upper hand in the struggle. McChrystal submitted a sixty-six-page report to the secretary of defense, Robert Gates, warning him that America was in danger of losing the war if more troops were not sent. He wanted to concentrate the deployment of additional forces in the southern and eastern provinces where the insurgency was most active.

He recommended an increase of thirty thousand to forty thousand troops.

Obama deliberated on McChrystal's suggestions for many weeks, seeking the opinions of members of his staff and some outside consultants. The debate went on for so long that policy planners who supported McChrystal's recommendations worried that Obama would miss the window of opportunity and act too late.

Opponents of the surge had their own reasons for not increasing America's commitment. Initially, they believed that the added $30 billion cost of the troop surge was a burden that the country could not afford in the midst of a struggling economy. Supporters countered that this amount of money was only 0.2 percent of the size of the entire economy in 2010 and was therefore affordable.

Another reason that opponents rejected the surge was that the stated goal of the war, defeating al Qaeda in Afghanistan, had been largely met by the summer of 2009, negating the need for adding American troops to the country. Instead, opponents argued that America should continue its pursuit of al Qaeda in other nations. They were a spent force in Afghanistan and incapable of mounting attacks against the United States on the scale of September 11. Former national security adviser James Jones noted that fewer than one hundred al Qaeda members were currently operating in Afghanistan and that they had "no base, no ability to launch attacks on either us or our allies."[54]

Opposition to the surge also came from those who were weary of a war that seemed to drag on with no conclusion in sight. In the spring of 2010, Operation Enduring Freedom became the longest-running war in which America had ever been engaged. Matthew Hoh, a State Department representative in Afghanistan, resigned on September 10, 2009, in protest over America's expanding commitment. Hoh wrote in his resignation letter that "thousands of our men and women have returned home with physical and mental wounds, some that will never heal. . . . The dead return only in bodily form to be received by their families."[55] This sentiment was shared by a growing segment of the American public.

Policy planners who had been calling for the surge since before Obama took office rejected the views of the opposition. They believed that by not boosting the undermanned U.S. forces on the ground in Afghanistan, America would suffer more troop casualties and a loss of the gains made thus far. Additionally, the troop deaths and casualties that had already been sustained would have been in vain. In the view of the surge supporters, the additional troops would halt insurgent advances and solidify allied gains. It would reaffirm America's commitment to supporting the Afghan government and people. It might also energize America's allies to reaffirm their own commitment to the coalition.

On December 1, 2009, Obama announced a planned increase of thirty thousand U.S. troops in Afghanistan. He also announced a withdrawal date for major American combat operations of July 2011. This timeline appeared to be unrealistically short considering the lack of progress that had been made in securing Afghanistan in the previous eight years. It also sent a mixed message that America was committed to supporting Afghanistan, but only for a limited amount of time. Lisa Curtis, senior research fellow for South Asia at the Heritage Foundation, a conservative policy research institute, writes that the withdrawal date "complicated U.S. efforts to inspire confidence among the Afghans, convince the Pakistanis to crack down on Taliban insurgents in their territory, and break the will of the Taliban who have calculated that they simply must wait America out."[56]

The Obama administration justified the withdrawal date by suggesting it would put pressure on the Afghan government to step up efforts to ensure a smooth transition to local security operations. Additionally, Karzai's relationship with the U.S. government had grown strained, further complicating matters. In December 2008, Karzai presented a list of demands to the U.S. government regarding troop conduct. He called for the limiting of military operations that put civilian lives at risk and damaged property. He also called for a greater respect of Muslim culture.

Gary Schmitt contends that the number of troops that Obama pledged to Afghanistan was not enough to meet the goal of ending the insurgency. He based his analysis on U.S. special forces doctrine, which maintains that the number of troops necessary to defeat an insurgency should meet a specific ratio compared to the population. The doctrine states that "twenty counterinsurgents per 1,000 residents is often considered the minimum troop density required for effective [counterinsurgency] operations."[57]

Schmitt writes, "By the fall of 2010, American force levels will be just shy of 100,000. Combined with allied and partner-nation contributions of some 45,000 troops . . . 134,000 Afghan soldiers and 109,000 Afghan national policemen, the total number of security forces will be . . . 280,000 troops short of

On December 1, 2009, President Barack Obama announced an increase of thirty thousand U.S. troops in Afghanistan and also set a withdrawal date of major American combat operations for July 2011.

Marjah: Caught Between Combatants

Control of some cities and regions in Afghanistan can bounce from the insurgents to the coalition forces and back again. Gary Schmitt, director of the Program on Advanced Strategic Studies at the American Enterprise Institute, explains one such instance in February 2010 in Marjah, a one-time Taliban stronghold in Helmand Province:

> With the Pentagon no doubt pressed to show results quickly and also not tie down Marines who could be used in other clearing operations, it declared the town effectively cleared after two short weeks. But attempts to turn the town's security over to Afghan forces and special police in the weeks that followed only resulted in the resurgence of Taliban activity, whipsawing the townspeople in a way that means it will take even longer to assure them that they should bet on their long-term security resting with the Afghan government.

In December 2010, the U.S. military command officially announced that combat operations in Marjah were completed, and after months of fighting, the district was free of insurgent activity.

Gary Schmitt. "Too Few Good Men." *Weekly Standard*, September 27, 2010, p. 10.

U.S. Marines prepare to enter a house in search of weapons in Marjah. In December 2010 the U.S. military announced that Marjah was free of insurgent activity.

meeting that 1:20 ratio for an Afghan population of about 33 million."[58] Thus, the thirty thousand troops that were pledged did not reflect the special forces guidelines for defeating the insurgency but was instead a reflection of the forces that America could spare at the time.

Schmitt's analysis was supported by a study conducted by the ISAF in early 2010. The study identified 80 key districts in Afghanistan in which the insurgency was operating at a peak level, plus 41 other districts of interest where the insurgency was present and could grow to a lethal capacity. Out of those 121 districts, the ISAF only had the resources to conduct operations in 48.

The Increasing Use of Unmanned Drones

Troops on the ground were not the only option available to the U.S. forces in combating the insurgency. Unmanned Aerial Vehicles (UAVs), commonly referred to as predator drones, had been a potent weapon in the American arsenal since 2001. These pilotless aircraft were flown remotely by troops far from the field of battle, and they served two purposes. The first was aerial surveillance and reconnaissance to locate and identify insurgent forces. For their second, and more potent purpose, the drones were armed with missiles, and they could strike targets with pinpoint accuracy that U.S. troops could not reach on the ground.

In 2009, when it became clear that Pakistan would not increase pressure on their side of the border, Obama began to significantly raise the number of drone sorties that were flown, and their increased use led to a higher number of kills in the field, including key insurgent leadership targets. CIA director Leon Panetta stated that drones were "the only game in town in terms of confronting or trying to disrupt the Al Qaeda leadership."[59]

Drones fit well in the light footprint strategy because they allowed U.S. forces to go directly after the insurgents without having to fight through the whole country in order to reach them. More than a dozen top al Qaeda leaders were killed in drone strikes in 2009. The use of drones has caused controversy, however. According to estimates by the New American Foundation, a public policy institute, the 233 drone strikes initiated

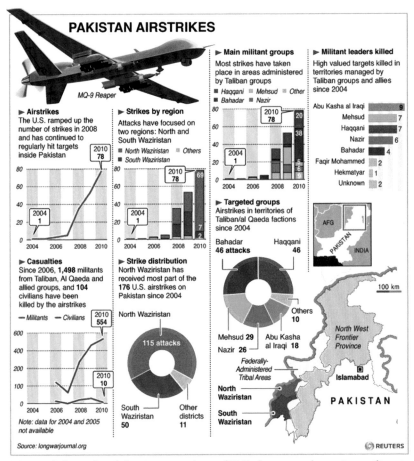

Map and charts detail the rising numbers of U.S. drone attacks against militants in Pakistan.

since 2004 killed between 290 and 470 civilians, approximately 21 percent of all drone-related deaths. In 2010 the number of civilian casualties dropped to 6 percent, but the use of drones in the skies of Pakistan has deepened the resentment that many Pakistani citizens and government officials have for the American presence.

Alternatives to Military Engagement

Opponents of the 2009 military buildup presented an array of options that relied on other efforts beyond military force. In their view, military force was too blunt and ineffective a tool to apply in fighting small terrorist groups that were highly mobile and capable of blending into civilian populations. Former deputy assistant secretary of state Celeste Gventer comments that "such an effort has but the faintest direct link to fundamental U.S. interests—preventing an attack on the American people and homeland—yet promises to be both exorbitantly expensive and fiendishly difficult."[60]

In January 2010 Afghan president Hamid Karzai announced his willingness to negotiate with moderate members of the Taliban by offering them a role in the Afghan government.

Instead of relying on the military, opponents of military engagement called on the United States to focus on other options, such as training and intelligence gathering. The United States could provide trainers and advisers for Afghan security forces, even though such efforts would not be able to secure the country in the near term. Intelligence-gathering efforts like aerial surveillance, covert operations, and intelligence sharing with the Afghan and Pakistani governments were already in place and only needed to be enhanced. Innocent and Carpenter note that

> since 9/11, America's capture of many high-level Al Qaeda operatives have stemmed from intelligence-collection, sharing, and cooperation with foreign governments. Al Qaeda . . . will not be defeated by amassing thousands of troops in Afghanistan. . . . By doubling down on the number of U.S. troops . . . the United States is giving Al Qaeda leaders exactly what they want: America remains mired in a protracted guerilla war, and U.S. tactics kill and alienate noncombatants, thereby facilitating terrorist recruitment.[61]

A more controversial alternative suggested by opponents of military engagement was to engage moderate members of the Taliban by offering them an opportunity to take a role in the Afghan government. Karzai announced in January 2010 that he sought to enter into negotiations with members of the Taliban who were not directly involved in the insurgency. His efforts demonstrated that elements of the Taliban were eager to take part in the government. A source close to negotiations between representatives of moderate Taliban factions and the Karzai government noted in October that the moderates "know that more radical elements are being promoted within [Taliban] rank and file outside their control. . . . All these things are making them absolutely sure that regardless of [their success in] the war, they are not in a winning position."[62]

There is concern among certain American policy planners, however, that negotiations with the Taliban will be counterproductive. Lisa Curtis and James Phillips of the Heritage Foundation write, "The goals espoused by the senior Taliban leadership and Al Qaeda do not differ enough to justify separating the two organizations with regard to the threat they pose to U.S. national security interests. If the Taliban increases its influence in Afghanistan, so does Al Qaeda."[63]

Despite its misgivings about the idea of reconciliation between the Afghan government and the moderate members of the Taliban, the United States will need to play a role in any negotiations that take place between the two factions. This will lend credibility to such discussions in the eyes of the skeptical Afghan public, and it may change the dynamics of the political situation in the country for the better. General David Petraeus, the U.S. and NATO commander in Afghanistan since June 2010, stated of attempts by the Taliban to negotiate, "This is how you end these kinds of insurgencies."[64]

Humanitarian and Economic Aid

Enhanced humanitarian and economic aid are also considered to be alternatives to military engagement. Direct aid and assistance in developing schools, hospitals, and a basic economy make Afghanistan a more stable nation and less in need of U.S. assistance over time. Curt Tarnoff, a specialist in foreign affairs with the Congressional Research Service, writes: "The U.S. program of assistance to Afghanistan is intended to stabilize and strengthen the Afghan economic, social, political, and security environment so as to blunt popular support for extremist forces in the region."[65]

Since 2001 the United States has provided approximately $52 billion in aid to Afghanistan, with some three-quarters of that money coming since 2007. Over half of all U.S. aid has been devoted to training and equipping the Afghan security forces. The second-largest portion of assistance focuses on national development efforts and development assistance programs. This includes a number of components, among them infrastructure—roads and public utilities like power plants, water filtration plants, and sewage treatment facilities. To this point the biggest successes have been in building roads and power plants. Over 1,650 miles (2,655km) of roads have been built, with a particular focus on

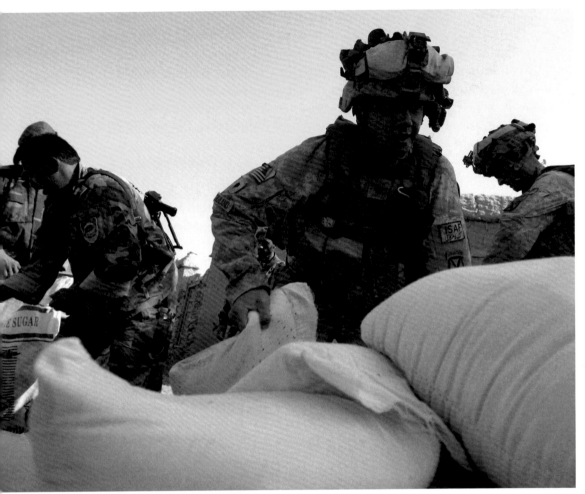

American soldiers deliver humanitarian aid to Afghans in Kunar Province. Since 2001 the United States has provided nearly $52 billion in humanitarian aid to Afghanistan.

the Ring Road, which spans the entire country. Construction of a 100-megawatt power plant in Kabul and the development of a power grid for major cities brought electricity to areas that have been without it for years.

The United States has initiated other programs for developing a legitimate business sector and the legal framework within which it can operate, including taxation and administrative policies.

Agricultural aid includes the establishment of food-processing facilities and veterinary units to take care of livestock. Programs dedicated to the expansion of access to basic health care included the construction of over six hundred clinics and the training of ten thousand health-care workers. Education efforts include the building and rehabilitation of schools, the training of more than fifty thousand teachers since January 2006, and the printing of millions of textbooks.

Stanley McChrystal Is Recalled

General Stanley McChrystal was recalled from Afghanistan by President Barack Obama and resigned his command on June 23, 2010, after he and his staff made disparaging comments about the civilian American leadership in a *Rolling Stone* magazine interview. In the June 25, 2010, issue, McChrystal or members of his staff called Obama adviser James Jones a "clown," and voiced skepticism about President Obama, Vice President Joe Biden, Ambassador Richard Holbrooke, and Ambassador Karl Eikenberry.

The most disparaging comments were made not by McChrystal, but members of his staff; however, military protocol is clear that a commander is responsible for the actions of those under his or her command. Andrew Bacevich, a professor of international relations at Boston University and a retired army colonel, analyzed the impact of the interview:

Obviously the war's not going well, nor is it apparently where General McChrystal himself thought it would be at this stage of things. But what stands out is the egregious lapse in professional conduct—not only on the part of McChrystal, but on the part of his subordinates. What this reveals is a command climate where expressions of contempt for senior civilian officials are permissible.

[While] frustrations [may be] understandable [the comments nevertheless represent] unprofessional behavior that is completely intolerable.

Quoted in Howard LaFranchi. "General McChrystal: *Rolling Stone* Story a sign of frustration?" *Christian Science Monitor,* June 22, 2010. www.csmonitor.com/USA/Foreign-Policy/2010/0622/General-McChrystal-Rolling-Stone-story-a-sign-of-frustration.

Another major U.S. project has been to provide assistance and education to expand the role of women in what has traditionally been a notoriously misogynistic society. This includes training women to take part in public service jobs, raising awareness of the legal rights of women, offering female health and reproductive education and services, and providing services for women who suffer mistreatment by husbands and/or male family members.

These aid programs must be monitored and held to specific benchmarks for measuring success, and establishment of realistic aid goals on a quarterly or yearly basis will be needed to keep track of the money. U.S. administrators also want to avoid letting the Afghan people become too dependent on American aid. If the Afghans came to believe that America would do everything for them, they would not likely take any initiative to better their own circumstances. Greg Mills, adviser to the ISAF, and David Richards, chief of defense staff of the British armed forces, write, "The international community's first priority is to find the means to make aid more than just a feeding trough for local warlords."[66]

Withdrawal: Pro and Con

The ultimate alternative to military engagement is a full withdrawal from Afghanistan. This is a hotly debated issue. Brian Michael Jenkins, senior adviser to the Rand Corporation, writes, "U.S. military withdrawal would leave Afghanistan in chaos, in which Al Qaeda and its allies, always resilient and opportunistic, would flourish. If further terrorist attacks did occur once U.S. troops were out, it would be even more difficult for them to return."[67] Innocent and Carpenter counter, however, maintaining that "instability, in the sense of a perpetually anarchic state dominated by tribal warlords and pervasive bloodshed, has characterized the region for decades—even centuries. Thus, the claim that Afghanistan would be destabilized if the United States were to decrease its presence is misleading, since Afghanistan will be chronically unstable regardless."[68]

These opposing views represent a larger argument over what the United States is doing in Afghanistan—defeating al

Qaeda and protecting America from terrorism, or stabilizing and rebuilding the country. These are distinctly separate goals, and supporters of withdrawal are not calling for an end to the fight against terrorism. Malou Innocent explains, "Rather than propping up a failed state, U.S. leaders should focus on countering the al-Qaeda threat still clinging to life in this region."[69] This would require following al Qaeda into Pakistan and leaving a large force of American soldiers in the area, which runs counter to the concept of withdrawal.

THE UNITED STATES CANNOT HELP AFGHANISTAN

"Given the nature of the conflict in Afghanistan, a definitive, conventional 'victory' is not a realistic option. Denying a sanctuary to terrorists who seek to attack the United States does not require Washington to pacify the entire country, eradicate its opium fields, or sustain a long-term military presence."—Malou Innocent and Ted Galen Carpenter, respectively, a policy analyst and vice president for defense and foreign policy studies at the Cato Institute, a libertarian think tank in Washington, D.C.

Malou Innocent and Ted Galen Carpenter. *Escaping the Graveyard of Empires: A Strategy to Exit Afghanistan.* Cato Institute, 2009, p. 1.

The July 2011 withdrawal date promised by Obama would not meet the expectations of those calling for an American pullout. Conditions for a drawdown of forces were based on an assessment of the military situation, and General Petraeus recommended a withdrawal that allowed for a continued strong combat role in Afghanistan.

A Legacy of Mixed Results

The stated U.S. response to the September 11 terrorist attacks was to bring the perpetrators to justice. Al Qaeda in Afghanistan was removed as a major force. Its sanctuary was smashed and several key members were either captured or killed. But

Osama bin Laden remained at large, believed to be hiding out in Pakistan, and al Qaeda cells still existed worldwide, continuing to plan and execute terrorist attacks, although U.S. intelligence managed to foil repeated attempts to strike against civilian and cargo airlines and heavily trafficked public locations. Other countries like Spain, Australia, and Great Britain were not so fortunate.

The Taliban government in Afghanistan was toppled for its role in supporting al Qaeda, but its removal from power actually turned out to be the easy part. It was accomplished in a matter of weeks, but ten years later, the United States still finds itself deeply committed to fighting an insurgency in which the Taliban play a major part.

WHAT ARE THE ALTERNATIVES?

"If the richest and most powerful countries in the world can't help this poor nation, God help us all!"—Unnamed Afghan security guard

Quoted in Obaid Younossi and Peter Dahl Thruelsen. "Afghan Progress Spotty but Hopeful." Rand Corporation, April 29, 2008. www.rand.org/commentary/2008/04/29/PJ .html.

From 2001 through 2010, the United States spent $400 billion on the war in Afghanistan. As of April 2011, the number of American soldiers killed in that war hit 1,520, with another 10,855 wounded. Some soldiers have returned from Afghanistan after paying the price of an arm, a leg, an eye, or more. A number of veterans suffer from post-traumatic stress disorder, and some have committed suicide. Additionally, veterans who have been unable to cope with their wartime experiences and/or the return to civilian life have been divorced, addicted to alcohol or drugs, and, in some cases, committed crimes.

Afghanistan now has a democratically elected government, but by 2010 it had yet to win the full confidence of the public due to ongoing corruption and the ineffectiveness of some of its agencies. The country had held two nationwide presidential elections by the end of 2010, but widespread accusations of voter fraud drew the legitimacy of those elections into question.

The United States, in combination with coalition forces and the new Afghan government, has done much to modernize Afghanistan and improve its badly decayed infrastructure, but the task is still daunting. International contractors and Afghan workers are engaged in a number of construction projects in several Afghan cities. Markets in these cities are stocked with goods, and shops are opening up in many locations. Much of this progress is confined to the north. In the south, progress is spotty, and the drug trade still flourishes.

The one constant in America's decade-long involvement in Afghanistan is the commitment that the United States has maintained to help Afghanistan become a stable nation. America's resilience in the war against al Qaeda was clearly demonstrated on May 1, 2011, after U.S. surveillance and information from a captured al Qaeda courier had confirmed that Osama bin Laden was located in a fortified compound in Abbottabad, Pakistan, 35 miles (56km) north of the capital city of Islamabad. The compound was in a small neighborhood less than 2 miles (3.2km) from a prestigious Pakistani military academy, raising serious questions among U.S. leaders, who had been told by the Pakistanis that they had no idea of Bin Laden's location. It was unclear how long he had been there, but his fortress included a multiroomed residence surrounded by a concrete wall at least 12 feet (3.6m) high and ringed with barbed wire. The compound was protected by several hardened al Qaeda fighters.

A U.S. Navy SEAL team, on Obama's direct orders, secretly crossed the Pakistani border from an air base in Afghanistan and entered the compound, killing Bin Laden and everyone else in the complex. Bin Laden's body and untold numbers of documents were taken from the compound. His identity was confirmed via facial recognition technology and, later, by DNA analysis. Bin Laden's body was flown out to the USS *Carl Vinson* in the North Arabian Sea, where he was given a simple Muslim funeral ceremony and then wrapped in a white shroud and buried at sea. Obama confirmed Bin Laden's death just before midnight on May 1, but also reaffirmed America's commitment

Osama bin Laden's compound in Abbottabad, Pakistan, is shown the day after U.S. Navy SEALs, in a daring raid, entered the compound, where they shot and killed the al Qaeda leader.

to the war that had started a decade previously. "The death of bin Laden marks the most significant achievement to date in our nation's effort to defeat al Qaeda," Obama said. "Yet his death does not mark the end of our effort. There's no doubt that al Qaeda will continue to pursue attacks against us. We must—and we will—remain vigilant at home and abroad."[70]

NOTES

Introduction: The Graveyard of Empires

1. Quoted in Christian Caryl. "Bury the Graveyard." *Foreign Policy*, July 26, 2010. www.foreignpolicy.com/articles/2010/07/26/bury_the_graveyard?page=full.
2. C.J. Dick. *Mujahideen Tactics in the Soviet-Afghan War*. Surrey, UK: Conflict Studies Research Centre, 2002, p. 3.
3. Quoted in George Crile. *Charlie Wilson's War*. New York: Atlantic Monthly Press, 2003, p. 224.
4. Quoted in Crile. *Charlie Wilson's War*, p. 516.
5. Quoted in Seth G. Jones. *In the Graveyard of Empires: America's War in Afghanistan*. New York: Norton, 2009, p. 48.

Chapter 1: Afghanistan Becomes a Terrorist Haven

6. Zalmay Khalilzad. "Afghanistan: Time to Reengage." *Washington Post*, October 7, 1996, p. A21.
7. Subodh Atal. "At a Crossroads in Afghanistan: Should the United States Be Engaged in Nation Building?" Cato Institute, September 24, 2003, p. 9.
8. Ahmed Rashid. *Taliban*. New Haven, CT: Yale University Press, 2000, p. 111.
9. Quoted in Jones. *In the Graveyard of Empires*, p. 82.
10. Crile. *Charlie Wilson's War*, p. 508.
11. Quoted in *Cato Handbook for Policymakers*. 7th ed. Washington, DC: Cato Institute, 2009, p. 498.
12. Quoted in Jones. *In the Graveyard of Empires*, p. 76.
13. Quoted in Jones. *In the Graveyard of Empires*, p. 83.
14. Quoted in *Frontline*. "The Man Who Knew." PBS *Frontline*, October 3, 2002. www.pbs.org/wgbh/pages/frontline/shows/knew/etc/script.html.
15. George W. Bush. Address to a joint session of Congress and the American people, September 20, 2001. http://georgew

bush-whitehouse.archives.gov/news/releases/2001/09/2001
0920-8.html.

Chapter 2: Operation Enduring Freedom Begins

16. Jones. *In the Graveyard of Empires*, p. 91.
17. Dalton Fury. *Kill Bin Laden: A Delta Force Commander's Account of the Hunt for the World's Most Wanted Man.* New York: St. Martin's, 2008, p. 287.
18. Charter of the United Nations. Article 51. www.un.org/en/ documents/charter/chapter7.shtml.
19. Marjorie Cohn. "Bombing of Afghanistan Is Illegal and Must Be Stopped." Jurist, November 6, 2001. http://jurist.law .pitt.edu/forum/forumnew36.htm.
20. Fury. *Kill Bin Laden*, p. 158.
21. Quoted in U.S. Army Sergeants Major Academy et al. *Long Hard Road: NCO Experiences in Afghanistan and Iraq.* Ft. Belvoir, VA: Defense Technical Information Center, 2007, p. 59.
22. Eric Blehm. *The Only Thing Worth Dying For: How Eleven Green Berets Forged a New Afghanistan.* New York: HarperCollins, 2010, p. 74.
23. Fury. *Kill Bin Laden*, p. 74.
24. Quoted in *60 Minutes*. "Elite Officer Recalls Bin Laden Hunt." Transcript. CBS News, July 12, 2009.
25. Paul Miller. "The Realist Case for Nation Building." *Foreign Policy*, September 23, 2010.
26. Quoted in Gary T. Dempsey. "Old Folly in a New Disguise: Nation Building to Combat Terrorism." Cato Institute *Policy Analysis*, March 21, 2002, p. 2.
27. Dempsey. "Old Folly in a New Disguise," p. 3.
28. Atal. "At a Crossroads in Afghanistan," p. 5.
29. Dempsey. "Old Folly in a New Disguise," p. 15.

Chapter 3: Attempting to Rebuild Afghanistan

30. Gary Berntsen and Ralph Pezzullo. *Jawbreaker: The Attack on Bin Laden and Al Qaeda.* New York: Crown, 2005, p. 219.
31. Malou Innocent and Ted Galen Carpenter. *Escaping the Graveyard of Empires: A Strategy to Exit Afghanistan.* Washington, DC: Cato Institute, 2009, p. 10.

32. Quoted in Jones. *In the Graveyard of Empires*, p. 112.

33. William Maley. *Rescuing Afghanistan*. Sydney: University of New South Wales Press, 2006, p. 60.

34. Atal. *At a Crossroads in Afghanistan*, p. 4.

35. Quoted in Anne Evans et al. *A Guide to Government in Afghanistan*. Washington, DC: World Bank, 2004, p. 14.

36. *House Committee on Armed Services Status of Security and Stability in Afghanistan*. 109th Cong., June 28, 2006 (statement of Karen P. Tandy, administrator, Drug Enforcement Administration). www.justice.gov/dea/pubs/cngrtest/ct062806 .html.

37. Quoted in Innocent and Carpenter. *Escaping the Graveyard of Empires*, p. 11.

38. Maley. *Rescuing Afghanistan*, p. 93.

39. Quoted in Jones. *In the Graveyard of Empires*, p. 125.

40. Maley. *Rescuing Afghanistan*, p. 131.

Chapter 4: Fighting the Insurgency

41. Quoted in Council on Foreign Relations. "Disillusionment in Afghanistan," November 17, 2009. www.cfr.org/publi cation/20770/disillusionment_in_afghanistan.html?bread crumb=%2Fbios%2F15575%2Fkim_barker%3Fgroupby% 3D0%26amp%253Bhide%3D1%26amp%253Bid%3D1557 5%26filter%3D280.

42. Quoted in Aryn Baker. "The State of Afghanistan." *Time*, August 21, 2008.

43. Hillary Clinton. *This Week with George Stephanopoulos*. Transcript. ABC News, November 15, 2009. www.state.gov/ secretary/rm/2009a/11/131939.htm.

44. *House Committee on Foreign Affairs U.S. Strategy in Afghanistan*. 111th Cong. April 2, 2009 (statement of Seth G. Jones, Rand Corp.), p. 4.

45. Crile. *Charlie Wilson's War*, p. 294.

46. Kenneth Katzman. "Afghanistan: Post-Taliban Governance, Security, and U.S. Policy." Congressional Research Service, February 18, 2011, p. 22.

47. Gary Schmitt. "Too Few Good Men." *Weekly Standard*, September 27, 2010, p. 11.

48. Jones. *In the Graveyard of Empires*, p. 323.

49. Quoted in Jones. *In the Graveyard of Empires*, p. 265.

50. Quoted in Rowan Scarborough. "Outlook Glum for 'Porous' Pakistan Border." *Washington Times*, December 5, 2010. www.washingtontimes.com/news/2010/dec/5/outlook-glum-for-porous-pakistan-border.

51. Katzman. "Afghanistan: Post-Taliban Governance, Security, and U.S. Policy," p. 49.

52. Stephen Biddle. "Interview: Obama's Afghanistan-Pakistan Strategy: 'A Reasonable First Step.'" Council on Foreign Relations, March 30, 2009. www.cfr.org/pakistan/obamas-afghanistan-pakistan-strategy-reasonable-first-step/p18982?breadcrumb=%2Fbios%2F2603%2Fstephen_biddle%3Fgroupby%3D0%26amp%253Bhide%3D1%26amp%253Bid%3D2603%26filter%3D280.

Chapter 5: Rethinking America's Commitment

53. Innocent and Carpenter. *Escaping the Graveyard of Empires*, p. 7.

54. Quoted in Doug Bandow. "Limits to U.S. Power in Afghanistan." Cato Institute, November 22, 2009. www.cato.org/pub_display.php?pub_id=11000.

55. Matthew P. Hoh. Letter of resignation to Director General of the Foreign Service and Director of Human Resources, U.S. State Department, September 10, 2009. www.washingtonpost.com/wp-srv/hp/ssi/wpc/ResignationLetter.pdf.

56. Lisa Curtis. "Administration Must Unequivocally Drop Afghanistan 2011 Withdrawal Date." Heritage Foundation, November 11, 2010. www.heritage.org/Research/Reports/2010/11/Administration-Must-Unequivocally-Drop-Afghanistan-2011-Withdrawal-Date.

57. U.S. Army and U.S. Marine Corps. *Counterinsurgency*. Washington, DC: Headquarters Department of the Army and Headquarters Marine Corps Combat Development Command, 2006, p. 1.

58. Schmitt. "Too Few Good Men," p. 10.

59. Quoted in Kenneth Anderson. "Predators over Pakistan." *Weekly Standard*, March 8, 2010, p. 20.

60. Celeste Gventer. "A False Promise of 'Counterinsurgency.'" *New York Times*, December 1, 2009.

61. Innocent and Carpenter. *Escaping the Graveyard of Empires*, p. 15.

62. Quoted in Karen DeYoung, Peter Finn, and Craig Whitlock. "Taliban in High-Level Talks with Karzai Government, Sources Say." *Washington Post*, October 6, 2010. www .washingtonpost.com/wp-dyn/content/article/2010/10/05/ AR20101005062 49.html.

63. Lisa Curtis and James Phillips. "Shortsighted U.S. Policies on Afghanistan to Bring Long-Term Problems," Heritage Foundation, October 5, 2009. www.heritage.org/research/ reports/2009/10/shortsighted-us-policies-on-afghanistan-to-bring-long-term-problems.

64. Quoted in DeYoung, Finn, and Whitlock. "Taliban in High-Level Talks with Karzai Government, Sources Say."

65. Curt Tarnoff. "Afghanistan: U.S. Foreign Assistance." Congressional Research Service, August 12, 2010.

66. Greg Mills and David Richards. "The Binds That Tie Us." *Foreign Affairs*, November 24, 2010.

67. Brian Michael Jenkins. "Afghanistan: A Marathon, Not a Prize Fight." Rand Corporation, October 1, 2009. www .rand.org/commentary/2009/12/01/RAND.html.

68. Innocent and Carpenter. *Escaping the Graveyard of Empires*, p. 6.

69. Malou Innocent. "Al Qaida Should Be Main Focus in Afghanistan." Cato Institute, March 29, 2010.

70. Barack Obama. "Remarks by the President on Osama bin Laden." White House, May 2, 2011. www.whitehouse.gov/ the-press-office/2011/05/02/remarks-president-osama-bin-laden.

DISCUSSION QUESTIONS

Chapter 1: Afghanistan Becomes a Terrorist Haven

1. What were the factors leading to the Taliban taking over control of Afghanistan?
2. What were the reasons al Qaeda gave for its war against the United States?
3. How did the United States determine that al Qaeda was responsible for the September 11 attacks?

Chapter 2: Operation Enduring Freedom Begins

1. What obstacles did U.S. forces face in relying on Afghan fighters in Operation Enduring Freedom?
2. What were the obstacles American forces faced in attacking the al Qaeda stronghold in Tora Bora?
3. What are the main reasons for and against nation building in Afghanistan?

Chapter 3: Attempting to Rebuild Afghanistan

1. What were the concerns about Hamid Karzai's leadership of Afghanistan?
2. What were the problems encountered in building the Afghan security and police forces?
3. What are the arguments for and against the total eradication of the poppy crop in Afghanistan?

Chapter 4: Fighting the Insurgency

1. What were the factors leading to the rising insurgency in Afghanistan?
2. In what ways did the "light footprint" strategy hamper early U.S. efforts to combat the insurgency?
3. What were the advantages and disadvantages of relying on Pakistan as an ally in the fight against the insurgents?

Chapter 5: Rethinking America's Commitment

1. How did the reliance on predator drone strikes aid the American counterinsurgency?
2. In what ways did Karzai split from the coalition?
3. What are some of the arguments for exiting Afghanistan in the short term?

ORGANIZATIONS TO CONTACT

Brookings Institution
1775 Massachusetts Ave. NW
Washington, DC 20036
Phone: (202) 797-6000
Fax: (202) 797-6004
Website: www.brook.edu

The Brookings Institution is a private nonprofit organization devoted to independent research and innovative policy solutions. It publishes numerous books and papers on current events and policies.

Cato Institute
1000 Massachusetts Ave. NW
Washington, DC 20001-5403
Phone: (202) 842-0200
Fax: (202) 842-3490
Website: www.cato.org

The Cato Institute is a libertarian public policy research organization —a think tank. Its scholars and analysts conduct independent, nonpartisan research on a wide range of policy issues, including government, economic, and foreign policy. It publishes journals, analyses, and papers regularly.

Department of Veterans Affairs (VA)
810 Vermont Ave. NW
Washington, DC 20420
Phone: (202) 273-5400
Website: www.va.gov

A cabinet-level department of the federal government, the VA is charged with providing benefits and services for American military veterans.

United Services Organization (USO)
PO Box 96322
Washington, DC 20090-6322
Phone: (888) 484-3876
Website: www.uso.org

Founded in 1941, the USO is a nonprofit group dedicated to providing morale and recreational services to military personnel, as well as goods and services for veterans and their families.

U.S. Central Command
7115 South Boundary Blvd.
MacDill AFB, FL 33621-5101
General public affairs: (813) 827-5895
Fax: (813) 827-2211
Media queries: (813) 827-6694 or -3208
Website: www.centcom.mil

The U.S. Central Command is headquarters for military operations in the Middle East and Central Asia, including Afghanistan and Iraq.

FOR MORE INFORMATION

Books

Deborah Ellis. *Off to War: Voices of Soldiers' Children*. Berkeley, CA: Groundwood, 2008. A series of interviews with children of soldiers deployed in Afghanistan and Iraq.

Alexander Klaits and Gulchin Gulmamadova-Klaits. *Love and War in Afghanistan*. New York: Seven Stories, 2005. This husband-and-wife team traveled through Afghanistan to study the lives of families and how they overcame extreme adversity.

Ronald E. Neumann. *The Other War: Winning and Losing in Afghanistan*. Dulles, VA: Potomac, 2009. The author, a U.S. ambassador with extensive experience in Afghanistan, examines how the United States was slow to comprehend the troubles it faced in that country and how the war in Afghanistan took a backseat to the Iraq War.

David Petraeus et al. *The U.S. Army/Marine Corps Counterinsurgency Field Manual*. Chicago: University of Chicago Press, 2007. This manual for U.S. military personnel is the result of collaboration among top U.S. military experts, scholars, and practitioners in the field, explaining and defining an approach to modern combat.

Gregor Salmon. *Poppy: Life, Death and Addiction Inside Afghanistan's Opium Trade*. Sydney: Random House Australia, 2009. An in-depth investigation into the opium trade in Afghanistan, including its impact on Afghan families who are tied to the trade: farmers, smugglers, police, and addicts.

Bob Woodward. *Obama's Wars*. New York: Simon & Schuster, 2010. The best-selling author and journalist draws on interviews, meeting notes, and documents to explore the decision-making process behind President Barack Obama's Afghanistan policy.

Videos

Camp Victory, Afghanistan (2010). This documentary, covering a three-year span, explores the difficulties encountered in building the Afghan army.

Motherland Afghanistan (2007). An Afghan-American filmmaker focuses on her father's efforts to rebuild hospitals in war-torn Afghanistan.

The Tillman Story (2010). A documentary about the family of American soldier Pat Tillman, who left an NFL football career to fight in Afghanistan and whose death by friendly fire in Afghanistan was covered up by the military.

Websites

Afghanistan Conflict Monitor (www.afghanconflictmonitor .org). An initiative of the Human Security Report Project at the School for International Studies at Simon Fraser University in British Columbia, Canada, this website highlights new research and analysis on the conflict in Afghanistan.

Afghanistan Crossroads (http://afghanistan.blogs.cnn.com). This blog by CNN provides updated information on America's presence in Afghanistan, as well as historical and cultural information.

Afghanistan: The Forgotten War (www.pbs.org/now/shows/ 428/index.html). The companion website to the PBS documentary about the Afghanistan war by the same title; includes video and additional information.

The Long War Journal (www.longwarjournal.org). A project of the Foundation for the Defense of Democracies, the journal provides original and accurate reporting and analysis of the so-called Long War (also known as the Global War on Terror). This is accomplished through its programs of embedded reporters, news and news aggregation, maps, podcasts, and other multimedia formats.

The Man Who Knew (www.pbs.org/wgbh/pages/frontline/shows/ knew). The companion website to the PBS documentary of the same title about John O'Neill, an FBI expert on al Qaeda who was killed in the attacks on the World Trade Center. It includes exclusive video, interviews, and a program transcript.

Rethink Afghanistan (http://rethinkafghanistan.com). This anti-war blog supported by the Brave New Foundation includes videos and other information dedicated to stopping the war in Afghanistan.

INDEX

PICTURE CREDITS

Cover: ChameleonsEye/Shutterstock.com

AP Images, 62, 72, 75

AP Images/Abdul Khaleg, 57

AP Images/Amir Shah, 38

AP Images/Anjum Naveed, 94

AP Images/Dominique Mollard, 26

AP Images/Ed Wray, 50

AP Images/Emilio Morenatti, 76

AP Images/Hermann J. Knippertz, 47

AP Images/Manuel Balce Cenata, 78

AP Images/MBC via APTN, 24

AP Images/Photography Plus via Williamson Stealth Media Solutions, file, 43

AP Images/Santiago Lyon, 20

AP Images/US Navy, Dennis Taylor, 30

Dimitri Kochko/AFP/Getty Images, 16

Goran Tomasevic/Reuters/Landov, 82

Ismael Sameem/Reuters/Landov, 69

Jean-Marc Giboux/Getty Images, 53

Keystone-France/Gamma-Keystone via Getty Images, 8

Kyodo/Landov, 58

Maps.com/Corbis, 10

Oleg Popov/Reuters/Landov, 88

Omar Sobhani/Reuters/Landov, 66

Reuters/Landov, 84

Robert Nickelsberg/Liaison/Getty Images, 13

Roger L. Wollenberg/UPI/Landov, 81

Romeo Gacad/AFP/Getty Images, 40

Vasily Fedosenko/Reuters/Landov, 33

Zhang Ning/Xinhua/Landov, 85

ABOUT THE AUTHOR

This is Richard Brownell's seventh title for Lucent Books. His other books include *The Fall of the Confederacy and the End of Slavery*, *America's Failure in Vietnam*, *The Oklahoma City Bombing*, *Immigration*, *The Cold War*, and *American Counterculture of the 1960s*. He is a published playwright with several stage productions to his credit. He also writes political commentary for various periodicals and websites. Brownell lives in New York City and holds a bachelor of fine arts degree from New York University.